STEP

STEPS TOWARDS EXTRAORDINARY POTENTIAL

STEP

STEPS TOWARDS EXTRAORDINARY POTENTIAL

SPENCER WOOD AND LEE SMITH

To Lisa and Jen,
Olivia and Jessica,
Rowan, Arthur and Oscar

We wouldn't be here without you

Our deepest fear is not that we are inadequate. Our deepest fear is that we are powerful beyond measure. It is our light, not our darkness, that most frightens us . . . And as we let our own lights shine, we unconsciously give other people permission to do the same.

Marianne Williamson

CONTENTS

FOREWORD

I first met Spencer in 2011 at a magic convention just outside of Gloucester. For those that have never experienced a magic convention, imagine 150 magicians of all ages and nationalities descending on a hotel for a weekend, to hear lectures from some of the world's best performers. However, the real 'magic' for me takes place in between sessions, as that's when I get to meet other magicians and share ideas and experiences, with the hope of leaving the convention with just one valuable 'nugget' that I can implement in my performances or my business for years to come.

Meeting Spencer was like a breath of fresh air. His warmth, energy and positivity got my attention straight away. We became friends almost instantly, and the more I learnt about him and how he ran his business, the more I liked. It is easy to see why he is one of the busiest performers in the country, as he is someone who truly cares about offering a quality product and fantastic service to his clients that go above and beyond those of any of his competitors.

I first heard of Lee because he had released some material for the 'magic community', which I had read. In 2012 I was hired by a company to be their 'trade show magician' at The Olympia Exhibition Centre, London. In essence, I would perform on their stand to help them generate a crowd and stand out from their competitors at the show. Lee was hired to do the exact same thing for one of their competitors . . . potentially a very awkward situation, as we would both be judged by our employers on who was bringing in the biggest crowds. I was nervous at the thought of going 'head-to head' against Lee – his reputation as one of best trade show magicians preceded him.

One hour into the five-day event, Lee walked straight up to me and introduced himself, with his hand outstretched and a massive smile on his face. With that single gesture, I knew the next few days would be absolutely fine. Over the course of the trade show we would meet up for coffee on our breaks, and during performances we would both tell our crowds to visit 'the amazing magician' on the nearby stand, to help each other out. Our employers loved it as we were sending more people to each other's stands and they were getting more leads than ever before!

Many other performers wouldn't have dreamt of speaking to their competition, let alone being nice! Lee's first impression was one of absolute class, coming from a confidence in his abilities, and it is something I have never forgotten.

Lee's approach to business and his core values were almost identical to Spencer's, and eventually I had the pleasure of introducing them and watching their business relationship flourish, as you'll hear about in this book.

Lee and Spencer are two of the UK's busiest magicians. However, I truly believe they would have been equally successful in any industry they'd have chosen, as they have a devastatingly powerful combination of a positive mindset and winning business processes, which they have finally agreed to share.

I wish this book had existed when I was starting my business! Enjoy.

Ben Hanlin – magician, television presenter and radio presenter

INTRODUCTION

Two magicians telling you how to succeed in business. We'll have to start by explaining why we're writing this book, to start to minimise any doubts you may have. By the final chapter, we hope that you will not only be fully on board, but that you will have started experiencing some extraordinary changes in your own life.

We had both already been very successful for a number of years, then enjoyed a massive surge in our energy and achievement levels when we started working together, approximately two years before writing this book.

We're not talking about improving our magic skills – this isn't about magic. We have found foolproof, straightforward and enjoyable ways to become significantly more successful in business. We're now running a number of companies, enjoying substantial incomes, and we have positive and ambitious goals for the future. And all that doing something that we enjoy.

We have spent many months meeting up, deliberating, researching and defining everything that has enabled us to get to where we are now, to empower *anyone* to take steps towards realising their own extraordinary potential.

We have both always been happy to share insight into our success with other people. Writing this book is a triple-whammy for us:

COLLABORATION

Helping other people to raise their game is mutually rewarding. Whether it's through indirect karma or direct payback is pretty irrelevant. Over the years, we have each helped other people gain new levels of success from sharing what we do, which has in turn helped us to increase our own CREDIBILITY, CONNECTIONS AND LEVELS OF ACHIEVEMENT. We have spent years finding out how to be successful; now we want to tell you how to do the same, in a much shorter time.

CONTENTMENT

There is an undeniable feel-good factor in helping others to achieve more and seeing the results they then enjoy. LIFE ENJOYMENT is just as important to us as making money; otherwise, what's it all about? We genuinely hope that this book will enable as many people as possible to reach new levels of success.

CONSEQUENCES

We both feel strongly that there is nothing to lose from other small businesses flourishing. At the time this book is first published, businesses in the UK have taken multiple blows, including from the economy, the taxman and the banks Despite all those factors, we have found WAYS TO MAKE OUR OWN BUSINESSES VERY SUCCESSFUL. We now gain great satisfaction from helping other entrepreneurs to increase their productivity and fuel the economy, in turn helping numerous other people to improve their standard of living. What is there to lose?

If you've read other books* about personal and business development, you've probably found them pretty long-winded. Core ideas and advice, padded out with examples, research and background information.

*If you haven't already read other books like this, you should. We'll talk about that more in Chapter 8.

You might even have read the first couple of chapters of a book then given up, or looked online for a summary of the main points.

This book is different. We'll give you a huge amount of condensed advice, broken down into easy-to-follow steps. You'll find some steps easy and others more challenging, but none will be impossible.

We have arranged the sections in a specific order – not through the life cycle of a business, but to deliver maximum benefit whatever stage of planning or business development you are starting from. In all, we want this to feel like an enjoyable journey, with even a few breaks thrown in.

We'll show you can expand your business, increase your income and make significant improvements to your work and personal life. You will very soon be able simply to start making changes based on what we say and enjoying the results. Even if you act on just one piece of advice from us and see improvements to your business, we will be satisfied that our book has been a success. And we feel confident that adapting our tips and tools to your own business will help you to enjoy significant improvements in your business and personal life.

We have included some PERSONAL STORIES – interviews with just a few of the people we've worked with. Everyone we have helped so far has given us 100% positive feedback, and the examples in this book will help you to a) understand how the same can work for you, and b) believe that what we say really works, that it is worthwhile you making the effort to follow our strategies.

It's up to you which parts you read, or which sections will make the biggest difference to you. You'll see from the introduction to each chapter whether it's an area you know you need to work on. But even if you're, say, already a monster networker, you will still gain from reading Chapter 4, if only to increase your own self-belief and your confidence that you're doing the right thing. We'll give you advice on how to improve your mindset, how to get in the game, and how easy and important it is to connect with the right people. We'll show you how selling your product or service can become a painless experience, and give guidance on managing the money side of your business. You'll learn how to improve your day-to-day business management, and how to keep making improvements and increasing your income. We'll teach you new ways of dealing with other people, about our fantastic buddy-up system and about how to reach further than you are currently aiming. STEPS TOWARDS EXTRAORDINARY POTENTIAL.

In less than two years before publishing this book, we have both established highly profitable businesses, doing what we enjoy most. It hasn't even felt like work. We've both had to learn fast and there have been setbacks – reading this will help you to avoid some of those, although some setbacks are an inevitable part of the journey. Running a successful business is always going to be at least slightly stressful, but we will help you to avoid some of the pitfalls and implement successful strategies, to reduce the stress and complications we have been through. What we do works – we're living proof of that.

There are too many factors involved for us to guarantee 100% success for every single reader. But if you follow all the steps we give, you will enjoy rewards you wouldn't previously have thought you could or would achieve. If anything doesn't work, get in contact – we want to help you work out why.

The biography normally comes at the end, for anyone who wants to check the author's credentials. We're starting with our stories, because it will help you to know from the start where we're coming from.

Lee Smith and Spencer Wood

CHAPTER 1
About us

We want this book to be personal, and we want to help as many likeminded people as possible to achieve new levels of personal and professional success. Before you start taking someone's advice, it helps to have at least some insight into their personal background. But you didn't buy this book to hear our life stories, so we'll keep it short.

You only need to know that it all started off pretty ordinary. Neither of us suffered hard times early on, neither of us excelled at school, neither of us started off in high-flying careers. The first question we usually get is how we got into magic, so we'll each start there. But remember: this book isn't about how to be a successful magician. It's about how anyone can apply new approaches and strategies to achieve more from any starting point, from gaining the courage to quit a 9 to 5 job, to running a global enterprise.

SPENCER WOOD

I was 27 when I first ever thought about learning some magic, after a family friend performed some tricks at our house. In 2001 I embarked on two years of magic lessons with the brilliant Robert Pound, then spent the next four years cutting my teeth as a performer. At the time, I was working full-time in sales, in the contract cleaning industry. I did well in sales – anyone who knows me will tell you I have a unique set of skills that allows me to talk with flare and passion, and my confidence in dealing with people gave me the edge. But I still faced a steep learning curve in how to be a successful performer – winning over a small group is very different from managing a room full of people.

My first big success in magic came in 2007, when I gained The Magic Circle's award for Close-up Magician of the Year. Later that year, I was invited to perform at Hollywood's prestigious Magic Castle. I'd made great progress in building my reputation and gaining confidence, but I still didn't quite have the guts to give up my day job. I managed two full-time jobs for nearly fifteen years.

It wasn't all plain sailing and there were of course some setbacks. Probably my worst experience was on 8 December 2012. I was performing the infamous 'Smash and Stab' trick at a wedding, in front of about 15 people. It's a form of Russian roulette and one of the most dangerous close-up tricks available. You have four cups covering four wooden discs, and one of the discs has a long, sharp, solid-steel spike sticking up from the middle. After the discs have been mixed up, the trick is to smash your hand down on each of the cups . . . apart from the one with the spike. And yes, this time I blew it – on my third hit, I slammed my hand down on the wrong disc. The spike passed instantly through my hand, severing nerves and tendons. I yelled out two words that no one should ever hear or repeat, threw the spike and disc from my hand (hitting one of the guests), made it to the corridor . . . and passed out. The only good news was that six of the guests were Kent paramedics, who probably saved my hand and my career. It took me a month to recover and return to magic.

I finally quit my job in sales, with its £50k salary, in June 2012. I know now I could have done it earlier, but I don't feel any regret – what's the point? It has been hard work since then to grow my magic business. But that's the thing: hard work isn't hard if it's something you enjoy doing, especially if you are earning a good income and feeling on top of your game.

Since I've started working with Lee, everything has moved up to completely new levels of success and increased income. First an overview from him, then I'll talk you through one of the most important themes of this book.

LEE SMITH

I was 18 when I bought a pack of see-through playing cards, just because I thought they looked cool. The same day, I happened to notice a book, *101 Amazing Card Tricks*, in a different shop. It felt like fate and I bought it. I might not have believed you if you'd told me then that I would one day be where I am now.

I'd hated school and couldn't wait to get out of there. After working for a while as a labourer for my dad, at the age of 19 I started running a pub. Soon I realised that, with a couple of attractive barmaids and a good chef, the business could just about run itself. I was the magic barman! I had the space to continue learning magic and put on shows at the pub, which got more popular as my confidence grew.

In 2010 I teamed up with another magician to produce a DVD, focusing on adapting a core number of tricks to work in any new environment. That is still a crucial factor for me – in magic and in business – that the simplest techniques can be the most powerful. While I had been successful in creating new tricks, this DVD was about using the most basic effects and adapting your personality to make the magic suit any type of audience. It soon became a bestseller.

In 2011 I produced another DVD, in partnership with a different magician. *iCandy* was even more successful in sales and reviews. Both DVDs gave me credibility as a successful and innovative magician, and I started to get enquiries from all the big magic clubs, including The

Magic Circle. I toured the UK lecturing in magic for a few years, acted as magic consultant for various TV shows, and continued to work full-time as a performer and in new areas, including trade shows. I was really satisfied with how far I had come and how successful I was. That was until I met Trevor Liley.

Over time, Trevor became my business mentor and helped me change my whole approach to business. You'll hear some of the brilliant advice he gave me as you read through this book.

Unfortunately, when Trevor first got in contact with me, I and my family were going through a really tough time. My beautiful wife, Jen, and I already had a three-year-old son, and were delighted when Jen fell pregnant with twin boys. But, as is often the case with identical twins, we faced some really challenging and scary complications in the months leading up to their arrival. We were eventually lucky enough to be offered pioneering surgery, which was thankfully successful, but in the meantime I'd had to stop taking on new work. We got plenty of support from family, friends and colleagues, but it was some time before I could get back to working full-time after the twins were safely delivered. After I had recovered from passing out in the operating theatre, that is!

I received two lifelines around that time that helped me get back up to full speed: the crucial advice and support from Trevor Liley, and work from another magician, Ben Hanlin. Ben needed to offload work because of a change in his career, so passed a load on to me. He also introduced me to Spencer Wood. Spencer always likes to have the last word, so he's going to finish off this chapter.

SPENCER AND LEE – THE BUDDY UP SYSTEM

Each of us is now enjoying awesome levels of success in business, and we've got stronger and ever-evolving plans for the future. While we'd both been successful before we met, it's only since we started researching for this book that we've realised how our collaboration has been the real game changer for both of us, personally and professionally.

The chapter about the Buddy Up System comes at the end of this book. That's because you will still achieve significant improvements by taking on all the advice before that chapter, with or without a business partner. Then, if you can also find someone you can work closely with to maximise your potential, Chapter 11 will help you to get there.

Thinking about how Lee and I have got here, it's almost as if our lives ran in parallel, until more and more coincidences brought us in line with each other. Our businesses were moving in roughly the same direction at about the same time, and I was even learning new tricks from the DVDs Lee had produced. Despite us living nearly 100 miles apart, our paths started to cross more regularly at business and social events. We hadn't been introduced, but you get that feeling when the same person keeps cropping up at the same place, and we soon started to realise when one of us had poached a client from the other. At that time, I was working closely with the brilliant magician Ben Hanlin, sharing work and contacts. In 2013 Ben's career changed direction, when he became the presenter of the new ITV show, *Tricked*. Ben knew Lee well and introduced us to each other, sort of handing over the torch.

It still feels almost unnerving how quickly Lee and I moved from casual social interactions to speaking every day, sharing ideas and developing new concepts and business directions together. We are very different in a lot of ways, as you'll see throughout this book, but there was an instant connection and level of trust that made it easy for us to work together very effectively. The fact that we bring different qualities to the table means that we are constantly learning from each other and sharing new perspectives, which multiplies the success either of us could have on our own. Lee and I now talk at least six times a day; our families are starting to wonder if we have a bromance going on.

Many years ago, someone told me something that stuck in my mind: 'You've probably already met your wife, you just don't know it'. That was shortly before I was at the Sandown Wedding Fair, where a woman returned to my stand to book me as the magician for her wedding. 18 months later that same woman, Lisa, rang to say their wedding had been cancelled. Three months after that, I had my first date with Lisa. We tied the knot a couple of years later and we are still very happily married, with two beautiful daughters.

While Lee and I were talking about our separate journeys, I laughed out loud when he said, 'Other people have probably already met their ideal work buddy, they just don't know it yet'. That may well be true for you. All the time you are reading this, keep your eyes and your mind open to who you could buddy up with. Then at the end of the book, we'll tell you all about our Buddy Up System.

CHAPTER 2

About you

You're probably wondering how we think we know anything about you, let alone enough to fill up a whole chapter. But what we'll tell you here applies to you and to just about every single person you know or will ever meet. Here's the short version:

MINDSET IS A GAME CHANGER – IT'S THE DIFFERENCE BETWEEN SUCCESS AND FAILURE. CHANGE YOUR MINDSET, AND YOU WILL INSTANTLY INCREASE YOUR POTENTIAL.

You know there are people who have won the lottery and then lost every penny. You'll have heard about others who started life with nothing and ended up multibillionaires. Mindset is nearly always the main – or the only – difference. Lottery losers are missing the motivation to (learn how to) retain their wealth. Rags-to-riches achievers dream the impossible and never give up believing that they can be successful.

Here's the first bit of positive news: YOU CAN MAKE THE DECISION AT ANY TIME TO CHANGE YOUR MINDSET, and you will start to see changes as soon as you do. Read this chapter to learn and believe how you can change your mindset now, and how that will help you to fulfil your potential. And, more importantly, how your full potential is much higher than you currently think it is.

UNLOCK YOUR MIND

Physical barriers can be insurmountable. If you are locked in a windowless room, there may be no way you can escape, as long as someone else has the key to the door. Mental barriers are different –

you are the only one that creates the barriers in your mind and you are always able to break them. You are always the person with the key.

A few years ago, Lee was told by his business mentor, Trevor Liley, that he should get a year's worth of income banked for the following year, before the year started, giving him guaranteed security for the year ahead. Without hesitation, Lee thought, 'That's impossible. It can't be done'. He considered the goal to be unachievable. Nobody that Lee knew – even the most successful magicians – booked more than a few months ahead. But at the same time Lee was thinking that, his mind had already accepted that the goal might actually be achievable and he'd started working out how it could be done.

Within two years, Lee had a year's worth of income booked in his diary for the next year. This was thanks only to the change in his mindset – if he had continued to think the goal wasn't possible, he would never have achieved it. He wouldn't even have tried. Not only that, but his new achievement had a massive knock-on effect. The goal he had once thought unachievable now became a concrete target. The increased confidence Lee felt, knowing he already had the year covered, gave him the tenacity to attract more bookings and stick to (or increase) his prices on anything new he took on. We now both get *at least* a year's income booked in our diaries for each following year, and are currently taking bookings for three years from now.

Like everyone, you already have hundreds of mental barriers determined by your background, your current circumstances and your levels of self-belief. You might have done badly at school, so feel sure you won't ever achieve as much as others. You may have a set idea in your head about how much people will pay for your service or product, giving you a limit on how much you charge. It's likely that you compare yourself with other people in your workplace or industry, believing you will never be as successful as them. The list is endless. If you think something is unachievable, you have set yourself a mental barrier. You won't go out and try to achieve the goal, because you don't consider it to be possible.

Believe this, for a start: EVERYONE, WITHOUT EXCEPTION, HAS HIGHER POTENTIAL. And as soon as you banish self-limiting barriers, you will start achieving that higher potential. Then, when you reach that new level, you simply need to reassess – you can always reach higher.

From this point forward, look out for any barriers you have in your mind and make the conscious decision that they are no longer valid. Think of all the levels you have set for yourself – the internal doubts and maximum targets – and write them off. Decide that you CAN achieve 10 times more than you've ever thought possible. It's irrelevant if you only reach 5 times as much – getting rid of the barriers in your mind will immediately get you on the way to achieving higher goals.

DON'T COAST

The vast majority of people become good enough at what they do . . . and then coast. They might be in a 9 to 5, doing well enough to come home at the end of each day feeling their job is pretty secure. They may have their own business, where they're covering their expenses but not bothering to keep thinking outside the box and pushing the boundaries.

For most people, it's only when something beyond their control changes – a crisis, say, when they face redundancy or lose a major client – that they are suddenly forced to reassess their potential in order to stay afloat.

WHY WAIT FOR THE CRISIS TO HAPPEN?

The only reason you are the person you are today, and not the person you would ideally like to be, is because you lack the motivation and/or the courage required to make changes. If you work for someone else, you only need to change your mindset and start applying yourself 100% to everything you do; you will soon make yourself indispensable to that company and be in line for promotion. If you are running your own business, as soon as you decide you are no longer happy with the level of income you have reached, you will be motivated to make the changes required to enable you to earn more.

It is very likely that now will never feel like the right time to take the plunge, to commit to full-time, self-employed work following your passion in life. Even if you do get to a point where you could consider it, the next morning something will change and you will again delay what you need to do. Even if you have at last made the decision that you are going to change your career, you might experience an unexpected setback and end up always tagging that decision negatively.

There will always be some disadvantages to being self-employed, which you will of course need to consider carefully, such as no automatic holiday or sickness pay. You will need to maintain success and make your peace on your own terms, not on anyone else's, about paying your bills, paying your living and making your business grow. We have both been through hard times, when we've felt stressed about not earning enough or that we're not busy enough. Right now, sitting here talking about it, it feels like we've won the lottery. We have learnt how to understand business, and we have worked hard enough to build up a fair amount of saved income. YOU CAN HAVE EVERYTHING YOU WANT, AS LONG AS YOU SET YOUR OWN GOALS AND TARGETS, AND WORK HARD TO ACHIEVE THEM.

It is important to focus on never feeling negatively unhappy with what you have achieved and are achieving. You MUST develop the mindset that you CAN do better and WILL do more, at every single stage of your life. Allow yourself to get out of survival mode and start enjoying the results.

CHOOSE TO FEEL GOOD

You have the choice on how you interpret any situation, and the option to make a positive change.

Here's an example. There will be times when you feel that something you've done hasn't gone well, that you could or should have done better. Then you have two options:

> ☹ **BEAT YOURSELF UP FOR DOING BADLY.**
> In that case, you will inevitably worry more and do worse next time you try to complete the task, if you haven't already decided to avoid ever doing it again.

> ☺ **MAKE THE DECISION TO THINK,**
> 'That wasn't the best one. It just wasn't right for me at that moment, but I'm still brilliant. I will learn from this and do it better next time.' You will then perform better next time round and be able to keep improving.

It might seem hard at this point to believe you can decide how you feel, to choose your emotions. But it really is that simple. You are the only one in charge of your mind, and you can change the way you feel about any situation.

Feeling good about your achievement is just as important. Even though you will always have higher targets, you need to remember to keep feeling good about what you have already achieved and how far you have already come. Here's a practical exercise that takes only a couple of minutes, which can really help in changing your mindset: at the end of each day, simply write down everything that's gone right that day. Whether you've secured a new contract, achieved a sales goal, heard from a client you hadn't been able to get hold of – whatever it is, write it down. At some point during that week, you'll have something that doesn't go well, but as long as you've already written down the things that have gone well, all of a sudden the setback won't feel nearly as bad.

Don't let yourself focus on what other people have. NEGATIVE ENERGY ABOUT OTHERS WILL ONLY HAVE NEGATIVE IMPACT ON YOUR OWN

PERFORMANCE. And anyway, there's no way you can know enough about someone else to know for sure how happy or fulfilled they are feeling. Think instead about how much more fortunate you are than the **vast majority** of people. Every step of the way, remember where you are and where you personally want to go, instead of comparing yourself with anyone else around you.

This is all about developing a positive mental attitude. We will go into more detail about the huge benefits of positivity, and how to achieve them, in the next chapter. For now, you just need to start letting yourself accept that you can choose to feel better about anything and that you mustn't beat yourself up when something doesn't go 100% to plan.

CHANGE YOUR MONEY MINDSET

It could be that money simply isn't as important to you as, say, helping other people or having time off. Hey, you have to define your own success on your terms, setting and aiming for your own goals in order to make your life better with regard to what is most important to you. You're the person who pays your bills at the end of every month. That said, we like to think that if you're happy now, you would only be happier with some extra income, especially if you then didn't have to worry about paying your bills. Whether you are 100% money-driven, non-materialistic, or anywhere in between, we aim to help you towards a more successful and positive mindset about money.

This includes helping you over a hurdle that might prevent you from aiming higher in the first place. A lot of people have a problem with admitting – even to themselves – that money is a main driving factor. We often hear things like 'I only need to be comfortable', 'I'm lucky, my partner will support me whatever I do', or 'Quality of life means more to me than money'. But you really don't need to feel bad about financial success, if only because it has a positive impact on the people around you and on the economy. Being successful in business is in itself personally rewarding. If you really don't need the extra income, you can use any financial rewards to help other people.

DON'T JUST SIT THERE

Of course, you can't just think positively and watch your business flourish. Developing the right mindset towards success will automatically get you doing things differently. But it works the other way round, too. Here are a few things you can start doing (NOW) to make changing your mindset even easier.

- **Whenever you have spare time, do something that has a positive effect on you.** For example, when you're on the train, read a book about business or personal development. If you don't take the train, subscribe to Audible (or any other audio app) to listen to books in the car or while you're walking. Everything you read or hear will have at least a small positive effect on your mindset and your performance levels, even if it's something you don't agree with and decide you need to avoid.

- **Get up earlier in the morning.** Make a start on this tonight, by deciding what you will definitely do with an extra 30 minutes tomorrow. Set your alarm to 30 minutes before you normally get up and leave your phone or clock out of reach, so you have to get out of bed to cancel the alarm. In those extra 30 minutes tomorrow morning, you could read something inspiring to get new ideas and better motivation for the day ahead. You might write a list of the things you are going to achieve during the day. You may decide to go for a run, to improve your energy levels before you would normally be starting your day. Whatever you do, you will be 30 minutes ahead of where you are every day at the moment, and you will feel positive about achieving more and changing your mindset. Then, a week after you're used to your new start time, bring it forward by another 30 minutes.

- **Decide to always arrive early at meetings.** You'll go in with a clearer head, not on the back foot or feeling stressed, and you will perform better. People will start to recognise you as more committed and reliable, and you will start enjoying the pay-off.

- **Start setting yourself at least one goal, every single day, and write it down.** We'll talk more about goal setting in Chapter 7, but right now is a good time for you to make a start, to get in the right mindset. Even if it's something small to start with, like calling a prospect or clearing your unread emails. At the end of that day, check back on the goal and congratulate yourself for achieving it. Then start thinking of what you'll do tomorrow – something slightly harder, or maybe two goals. You will very soon start feeling a greater sense of achievement and have a more successful mindset.

- **Get into a strict habit of keeping on top of emails and phone calls.** Once you are in the habit, it will feel easy to respond quickly to each email or call, and you will feel less negative stress. Remember, every single communication you receive is in at least some way very important to the other person, so they will feel respected when you respond in good time. The rewards far outweigh the time it takes you to fire off an email or pick up the phone. We'll be giving more specific advice about dealing with calls and emails in Chapter 8.

- **Take time to research people you are going to meet.** After the meeting, make quick notes about what you've discussed, including anything personal they told you, then refer to the notes before you next see them. Showing a personal interest in a company and in other people will increase mutual respect tenfold. The benefits far outweigh the small investment of time you have made, and you will love the results.

- **Start considering everyone you meet slightly differently.** Look at each person as an investment, as future work, a colleague, or a client. New business and significant relationships will start to develop automatically, just because you are applying a different mindset. You can read more about this in Chapter 4.

- **Arrange ad hoc meetings with colleagues and business peers** – you will automatically pick up new ideas and develop vital connections. Aim especially at contact with anyone more successful than you. Here's a concept we will come back to later in the book: IF YOU ARE THE MOST SUCCESSFUL PERSON IN THE ROOM, YOU ARE IN THE WRONG ROOM. We'll tell you more about the importance of making connections in Chapter 5. For now, just believe this: when it comes to connections, more is always more – you have nothing to lose by meeting up with anyone, even if they don't relate directly to your job or line of business.

These are just a few examples of the positive actions that will help you towards a more positive mindset. Your new mindset will allow you to achieve more, which will raise your success levels . . . and motivate you to take more action. This is the opposite of a vicious circle – we call it the **MAGIC VORTEX**. You'll see an image of this on the next page, and ten other examples of the **MAGIC VORTEX** throughout this book.

We hope this chapter has already inspired you to start to make changes. Maybe you've taken a couple of days to read this far and have already started to get rid of any internal barriers you have set for yourself, to feel more positive or to take actions to help you to change your mindset.

Here's the most important part of this chapter: WHENEVER YOU DO START TO SEE REAL CHANGES, DON'T GO BACK TO COASTING. Let your new mindset become your new identity, so that you stay in the habit of working towards achieving ever-higher potential. You can and will start to enjoy levels of success you hadn't previously thought possible.

THE MAGIC VORTEX

FEEDBACK FROM DEAN WHITE
VIDEOGRAPHER – WHITEPARTRIDGE MEDIA

I first got to know Lee about three years ago when we met working at a wedding together. We stayed in touch, meeting up now and again for a chat about business in general and talking about collaborating on film projects.

One morning I bumped into Lee at a local supermarket. I was at a low point in terms of my work and he was just setting out on a new adventure of helping businesses grow. Standing next to the pickles and table sauces, we had what would turn out to be a lifechanging chat.

In the coffee chats that soon followed, Lee helped me completely change the way I was approaching my work. I went from having an empty calendar to snowed-under in a matter of weeks! It was all about changing my mindset. Where am I holding myself back? Am I doing enough? Who are the voices around me and are they helping or hindering? Am I just accepting things or am I making things happen?

From learning just some of the very basics from Lee, I developed a sense of self-belief that I lacked previously. This fed a confidence and a drive forward to change my habits, and things just started to happen. From contacting old clients and following up on every lead, new and unexpected pathways would appear.

I don't want to sound vague but it really has been all down to just changing my mindset. Taking total responsibility for your situation and taking action is the only way. And the good news is, there's tons still to learn!

CHAPTER 3
100% positivity

Before you start reading this chapter, go back and reread the interview at the end of Chapter 2. Even if you have only just read it, take a couple of minutes to fully absorb what Dean White recently told us.

Dean is a brilliant videographer and was already running a successful business. He and Lee knew each other from the wedding circuit, but it was a chance meeting in a supermarket that led to a whole new approach for Dean. Lee told Dean about some of his ideas; they decided to meet and talk more, and were soon arranging regular meetings to share business strategies. And Dean is 100% convinced that the biggest difference came from changing his mindset, based on what he had discussed with Lee.

In the last chapter, we explained how you can get going in the right direction in developing your own mindset to allow you to achieve more. Now we need to complete the circle, showing you what a positive mindset can help you to continue to achieve, every single day. There are unlimited sources of research, books, talks and scientific proof about the benefits of a positive mental attitude, if you ever have time or feel the need to research further. We are going to tell you about THE EIGHT MOST POSITIVE CHANGES we have made to become more productive in everything we do, to get us where we are today.

THINK BIG

In our STEP System Seminars, it is incredibly gratifying to see people's reactions when they uncover opportunities they wouldn't otherwise have considered. For you, now, please just do this: GET INTO THE HABIT OF ASKING YOURSELF AT ALL TIMES – WHATEVER YOU ARE DOING, WHEREVER YOU ARE, WHOEVER YOU ARE WITH, WHATEVER YOU ARE WATCHING OR READING ABOUT – HOW YOUR BUSINESS COULD FIT INTO THAT AREA.

Don't focus only on what you are already doing. Think about how you could adapt your product or service to become something indispensable to someone else in a completely new environment.

There will be a multitude of ideal business openings you just haven't ever thought about. Here's an example. We are both magicians, which makes it obvious that we work as performers. When you think of a magician, you probably picture someone performing on a stage, or you may think about a celebrity close-up entertainer. A few years ago, it was almost unheard of to have a magician at a wedding . . . now it's an obvious and rock-solid market for anyone in our profession. Weddings are a reliable source of income for us both, and nothing beats the feeling of receiving a review from a couple, thanking you for making their whole day enjoyable and unforgettable.

Then why would someone hire a magician to represent their company at a trade show, or for a product launch? How could a magician transform a corporate team-build event or deliver sales training? We won't answer those questions here – you'll find out more as you go through this book. The point now is that THINKING OUTSIDE THE BOX has opened up numerous markets for us.

Open your mind, think about any new markets that would be profitable for you, and let your mind start to find ways to get you there.

GET OUT OF YOUR COMFORT ZONE

Whenever you have uncovered a new opportunity, you need to make the positive decision that you are going to do whatever is required to achieve it. This is one of the most important points in the whole book: YOU HAVE TO GET USED TO LIVING OUT OF YOUR COMFORT ZONE. IN ORDER TO MAKE REAL PROGRESS, YOU MUST CHALLENGE YOURSELF AND ACCEPT THAT YOU ARE GOING TO HAVE TO DO THINGS THAT YOU DON'T YET KNOW HOW TO DO.

This doesn't have to feel daunting – you don't have to do things you *hate* doing – you just need to push yourself to do something you don't usually do, which you might at first not feel 100% comfortable about. Here's the best bit: after you have worked outside of your comfort zone for a short time – in a couple of jobs, for a few new clients – you will have created a NEW COMFORT ZONE, because it will no longer feel difficult to be working in that new area. Not only that, but you will feel fantastic about what you have achieved; there aren't many things in life that are more rewarding than being successful at something new and challenging. And it is self-perpetuating – it's the *MAGIC VORTEX*. You will have gained income, achievement and confidence. It is almost inevitable that you will already be looking for other new opportunities, this time not feeling as anxious at the prospect of getting out of your comfort zone. Everything will already feel much more achievable, fuelling your positive mindset and giving you the confidence to look for new things to try. The most successful people we know are the people who are always operating outside their comfort zones. Some people say they have an internal target for how far they can keep pushing the boundaries before they just can't do something. They're always going beyond what is comfortable to them, so that they can expand.

If you're really unsure about entering a new environment and are worried about taking the first step, consider offering your product or service for free. If possible, turn it into a bonus in order to convert another sale. Delivering something for nothing allows you to perform and/or sell more confidently, then it won't be long before you can feel confident in selling the service or product at full price.

BE CONTENT

Money used to be the only driving force for both of us. After all, we wanted to be more successful in business, and money felt like the only obvious measure of success – it isn't unusual for money to be the main driving force, especially for entrepreneurs. We are not saying that you shouldn't be trying to earn more . . . THE CRUCIAL FACTOR IS HOW YOU FEEL ABOUT WHERE YOU ARE.

Spencer one day realised that feeling negative about other people having a better car or a bigger house was having a negative effect on his own performance, so he decided to turn the situation around. He started off by getting up every day and writing down five things he had that somebody else didn't have. That he was healthy, had a roof over his head, that he had signed a deal with a new client – whatever he was feeling best about at that time – and he noticed significant results within days. He felt more positive, he performed better . . . and his income increased.

You don't need to try to change your personality overnight. Don't beat yourself up if you find yourself feeling jealous when someone tells you about a load of new business they have achieved or the amazing holiday they've just booked. But once you have made a conscious decision not to worry about what other people have, it will become easier and easier to let any negative feelings go. You could decide instead to use someone else's success to help you realise that more is possible, and use it as motivation to earn more yourself in the coming month or year. Ultimately, even that won't be necessary – you can decide to judge your own success purely on your own terms, not on what anybody else does. You'll be able to start to see the bigger picture, the bigger goals, the bigger plans . . . for yourself.

Over the next few days, take note of any negative emotions you have when you are comparing yourself with other people, and simply make a conscious decision to turn those emotions around. Feeling bad about what other people have will only make your life harder – you will be so focused on what they are doing and achieving that your own performance will be weakened. And there will always be someone in front of you, no matter what you achieve. Write a list of things you have, the reasons you have to feel good about what you have. Set yourself your own targets, regardless of whether they are above and beyond what someone else has, as long as they are above and beyond what you have already achieved.

There is no doubt that money is still a driving force for both of us. We are both ambitious and have set ourselves very high long-term financial goals. But we love performing and entertaining people, and it feels a massive improvement to be enjoying our work for what it is, on our own terms.

ELIMINATE NEGATIVITY FROM OTHER PEOPLE

Negative people really drag you down, and your reduced positivity has an impact on anything else you do. You must already have noticed the difference in your mood after you've been speaking with a glass-half-empty friend, compared with how you feel after meeting up with someone who is positive and sees nothing as a real or lasting problem. Straight after that positive meeting, you'll have a smile on your face and feel more buoyant and positive about your own life and your business. And you know the difference that a confident vibe can make to just about any other situation you are faced with.

It's great for us when we receive responses from people who have implemented something we've suggested, then got in contact to tell us about the improvement it's made to their business. We haven't ever had comments to say people have experienced adverse effects. We have, however, over the years received negative comments on social media, from people telling us that we post too much or that what we're suggesting won't work. They want us to stop doing what they don't even want to begin to do, to make them feel better about not doing it. We will normally still encourage them to at least give it a try, rather than just feeling negative about it. If that doesn't work, we'll tactfully suggest they stop following us on social media.

We have both seen increases in our business income and general wellbeing since we started to remove the negative people from our lives and focus on hanging around with the more successful people. YOU ARE WHO YOU WALK WITH. And remember, people only don't want you to do something if it's something they're not doing themselves.

Wherever possible, you need to learn to reduce contact with anyone who saps your energy. The family member who doubts your ability, the associate who is standing still with their own business, the friend who puts a gloomy spin on everything. Avoid any significant amount of time with anyone like that, and spend time instead with the people you know who have positive energy and high aspirations. Even in the relationships where you do have a lot of faith and trust, there can still be an element of negativity. You don't need to cut ties with that person, but sometimes that stuff needs to be aired, so that you can get back into the right place with them.

We love this quote from the hugely successful American actor and comedian, Kevin Hart: 'Don't invite doubters into the conversation. You already know what you want to dedicate yourself to, so you don't need to ask for their approval. There's no need to seek external approval when you already have internal approval.'

EMBRACE NEGATIVITY

Everyone has ups and downs, and you don't have to pretend everything's always perfect. There's no escaping the fact that you'll go through phases when business is slow or you experience setbacks in your personal life. There will also be times when, even though in theory everything's fine, you can't help feeling less motivated or optimistic than you normally would. These are all times when it's best to embrace negativity, accepting it as a normal part of everyone's business and personal life.

Here are three points you can refer to whenever '100% positivity' feels impossible:

- **Some negativity is inevitable.** If you feel guilty for not feeling positive, you'll only fuel the negativity. Simply accept that it's completely normal to feel less positive at times.

- **Negativity usually comes in cycles**. As soon as you can accept that this current dip is only temporary, you'll be able to relax and look forward to the next positive stage of your life cycle.

- **Negative emotions can even benefit your productivity.** Feeling angry or frustrated can make you more determined and more creative in finding a solution. Some stress can increase your energy levels, and you can use any disappointment in what you're achieving to motivate you to achieve more. In short, whatever type of negativity you are feeling, we feel sure that you can turn it into a positive.

You've probably already noticed the main emphasis here, on accepting what you are feeling. Trying to completely resist and deny negative feelings only serves to make them more real and/or intense.

There's a simple exercise that backs this up. Close your eyes, and try not to picture a red bus.

If you did just do as we asked, we'd bet anything that you failed. You'll have pictured little other than a big, red, double-decker bus, right in front of your eyes. It's how our brains work, and it demonstrates how futile it is to try and resist or deny negative feelings. Acceptance forms the basis for most successful meditation practices, including mindfulness, which encourage you to experience negative thoughts and emotions without feeling bad about them.

Acknowledging and embracing a temporary and healthy level of negativity will make it easier for you to work towards your even healthier and more productive positive state of mind.

BELIEVE IN YOURSELF

We're not going to tell you again how it is possible to choose how you are feeling – hopefully you have already taken that on board. If you have already started changing how you feel, to be more positive, consciously congratulate yourself now on making some seriously important progress. Either way, we need to tell you now about how you can make a conscious decision to feel more confident.

You will already have noticed that you do better when you are feeling more confident. When you are having a good day – say when you've had some great news, or when you are doing something you have practised often – you perform better at whatever you are doing. That in turn increases your confidence . . . it's another *MAGIC VORTEX*.

No matter how well you are doing now, decide to keep reminding yourself that you are good at what you do. Whether you are feeling negative about how you are performing, or feeling on top of your game, make the decision now that you are going to do it better tomorrow. As soon as you start increasing your levels of self-belief, you will push harder, perform better at work, deliver more confidently, make more sales, increase your prices . . . and your confidence will grow.

DO IT

In a chapter on 100% positivity, you might be surprised that we're telling you:

IT ISN'T EASY TO BE SUCCESSFUL IN BUSINESS.

But hey: THAT DOESN'T MEAN IT ISN'T ENJOYABLE.

You'll have heard entrepreneurs saying how hard you have to work to be successful in business. We're not denying that – you have to work hard to be successful in anything. But if you embrace and value the fact that you are (or will be) doing something you enjoy, you will enjoy the hard work and challenges, along with all the personal and financial rewards.

We both find it sad when we meet people who have a hobby they really love but don't quite have the courage or conviction to turn that hobby into their main source of income. We hope to inspire as many people as possible to take the plunge, to know that they can follow their passion and make money out of it. You've got to work really hard to make it work, but the reward will be worth it. If you wait for a crisis, like being made redundant, you might never get there. THE TIME MIGHT NEVER FEEL RIGHT.

When do you ever have a month of really low outgoings, when you feel financially secure enough to take action that feels riskier than the job you are doing now? Sure, we both ran two full-time jobs for a while before we bit the bullet. While we've each decided it's a waste of energy to feel regrets about that, it's a fact that we could still be years ahead of where we are now.

We want our experiences to encourage as many people as possible to take the leap and start enjoying the outcomes as soon as possible. If you are telling yourself that you will get everything in place now and that you will be ready to launch your business in six months, we would be willing to place a bet that you will be saying the same six months from now. If you want some inspiration about how going self-employed could work for you, read our interview with Andy Larmouth, at the end of Chapter 7.

We have now both developed clear, positive and proactive mindsets. We've decided that if we don't act on our convictions now, it probably won't happen. We no longer (ever) let ourselves sit and think 'Maybe I'll do it next year'. Even if we do get around to it next year, we'll be a year behind where we could have been. The difference this mindset makes to our productivity is astounding. **Whatever it is you wish you were doing, you need to make a decision and go with it.**

There's a brilliant book that takes this one step further: *The 5 Second Rule*, by Mel Robbins. Mel's one-liner description: 'If you have an impulse to act on a goal, you must physically move within 5 seconds or your brain will kill the idea.' Make a decision, then say to yourself '5-4-3-2-1 – ACTION' – and just do it. You don't leave yourself the option of not acting on your decision. Since reading the book, we are both finding it easier to get a lot more done in a lot less time. *The 5 Second Rule* also covers topics like developing your self-confidence and breaking the habit of procrastination. If you are finding it hard to think of a reason to get up early, why not buy the book then start setting your alarm earlier just to read it? After you've finished this one, that is.

NEVER STOP DOING IT

PROACTIVITY IS KEY TO EVERYTHING WE DO. We have realised that, in order to keep growing, it is essential that we keep generating new ideas and new thought processes. We don't have any chill-out time – time out to do nothing – because we are always thinking about the next project. If we didn't think like that, we wouldn't be doing what we are now. Constantly thinking of new ways to grow enables you to get ahead of your business, instead of behind it. The further ahead of the game you get, the better.

Proactivity on a daily basis is just as important as the bigger picture. It's no good simply looking for things to be busy with, or ways to make yourself look busy. It's actually much easier than that: as soon as you develop a proactive mindset, you will find yourself productively busy all of the time.

With three young children, including super-active twin boys, Lee recently realised he needed to employ a childminder for one day a week, to give him extra work time. That could also have given him a chance to relax . . . but Lee made the conscious decision that he needed to be more proactive than ever. He made the effort to set up valuable meetings on that day each week, to gain more business than he would normally, to generate the extra income specifically to pay for the childminder. Within a short time, the extra business he gained on those days enabled him to pay for full-time childcare during work hours. Lee acknowledges that he is now in a position where he can have a day off if he wants to, but he hardly ever does. Even when he does have a free day, he keeps doing something related to running his business or generating more income.

Neither of us uses an alarm – we just wake up early. Then we don't lie in bed thinking about stuff – we know what we want to do, so we get up and get on with it. We know there will be a lot of people reading this thinking that feels impossible. Maybe you are used to saying that you are 'not a morning person'. Or you may have found another way to justify staying in bed for longer, like 'There's no point getting up early, because the people I do business with aren't around then'. As soon as you can change your mindset, to decide you are going to be proactive and always to look for positive ways to grow your business, you will start to find reasons to get up earlier than you do now, and to enjoy doing it.

No one pretends that there are no stresses involved in being successful in business. But the more successful you become, the less those stresses will bother you. YOU'LL EVEN BE ABLE TO START ENJOYING THE STRESSFUL PARTS, KNOWING THAT THEY ARE ONLY CHALLENGES THAT YOU WILL OVERCOME. And here's the most important part: being proactive helps you to combat stress. Spencer, for example, has recently started to experience a great new state of mind. His head is normally jam-packed with ideas, thoughts, plans, mental reminders, etc. In the last few months, he has found times when he is sitting thinking – say, on a train or at his desk – where he can 'see' white space in his head. A calm, empty space, with no issues – a beautiful place to be. Spencer is convinced it is because he is doing so much at the moment, reading and developing his business, that he can relax and enjoy positive mental respite when time allows (even if his subconscious mind is still occupied in working out ways to reach the goals he's already set).

Being proactive – making the decision to never stop doing what you want to succeed in – is a state of mind that will guarantee you achieve more. Here are a few other simple ways you can help yourself to develop a proactive state of mind:

- **Stop having negative conversations.** We all have worries, and things that feel unfair or negative in our lives. Talking regularly about those worries will magnify them in your mind and make you feel less positive and less proactive.

- **Don't dwell on setbacks.** Everyone has rough days and quieter times in business. Keep focusing only on what you want to do and how you are going to do it. Focus on the prize, and you will see positive things start to happen.

- **Apply this sequence to anything you want to do:**

DECIDE, COMMIT, ACT, SUCCEED, REPEAT

That's no new concept from us, but it is one that works and that we always use. Make your decision, commit to it, act on it, be successful at it, then repeat that process all over again. Write those five words out clearly and stick them up somewhere where you keep seeing them and keep genuinely acknowledging what they mean. Then make sure you start to adopt that way of approaching anything you want to achieve.

One of the most positively minded people we know is the psychological magician, Sylar. He's so outgoing and upbeat, it's hard to imagine him having a bad day. But Sylar has told us about a six-month period where he dreaded every gig and felt trapped by his job and its commitments, despite his overriding passion for magic. It happens to all of us, and it was a relief to hear that even Sylar had experienced the same. He tackled his temporary lack of motivation in two ways: buddying up and mindset.

Sylar approached Steve Rowe, a magician and graphic designer who lives near to him. Steve is always in a good mood, embraces any new challenge, and his creativity makes him the most innovative and inventive magician we know. He and Sylar hadn't even heard of our Buddy Up System when they started working together; we hope they benefit from reading more about that in Chapter 11. Sylar and Steve together will fill an empty warehouse with their positive energy, so their collaboration gave Sylar his final push out of his six-month stagnation.

Before buddying up with Steve, Sylar says that the critical factor was simply deciding to change his mindset. He forced himself to think positively, knowing that otherwise he would end up hating what he loved doing most. He allowed extra time to sit in his car before every gig, to give himself a positive pep talk. He told himself that he loved what he did, that he was going to be brilliant, and that every audience member would think he was fantastic. Sylar simply decided that he needed to make this work for him and get back to his old levels of enthusiasm and energy. You only have to have five minutes with Sylar or Steve now to see how ridiculously positive they are about everything they do.

In the previous chapter, we gave you this statement: **Mindset is a game changer – it's the difference between success and failure. Change your mindset, and you will instantly increase your potential.** If you still have any doubt about that statement, take time to access other sources to put your mind at rest.

If you are already on board, please still keep coming back to these two chapters, to remind yourself of all the positive reasons and easy steps you need to remember and act on. There's a good reason we needed to start with mindset. The rest of the book will cover the strategies you need to achieve success, but it is 100% vital that you believe and absorb these two chapters first, in order to gain maximum effect from the rest of the advice we give you.

Don't be put off from reading the rest of this book if you're not yet running your own business. It could be even more beneficial for you to learn more now, to give your new enterprise a rock-solid foundation. We're not going to keep on at you to ditch your day job – ultimately, that decision has to be yours. But whenever you do, please remember how important it is to keep getting out of your comfort zone, generating positivity, eliminating negativity and always believing in yourself. Chapter 4 will tell you how to create MASSIVE IMPACT whenever you do join the game.

CHAPTER 4

Game time

If you think that business is purely about investment, technology, numbers, processes and marketing, think again. BUSINESS REVOLVES AROUND PEOPLE. People are the ultimate consumers of every single product and service that has ever been created, and people make every single decision about what is purchased, how and when. Even if you already have an excellent product or service, even if you're brilliant at sales, no one's going to buy from you if they don't know who you are. In this chapter we are going to share our tips on how to make a lot of new connections and to make sure they work for you.

We'll start with something that feels laborious to most people: networking. It is one of the most important things you need to do if you are running a business, but it can be boring, intimidating and time-consuming. Even the word 'networking' feels negative to a lot of people. Until you take a completely new approach . . .

NON-STOP NETWORKING

There must be some value to networking meetings. Maybe we didn't go to the right ones, but the few either of us has attended weren't very productive or rewarding. They went something like this:

1. Turn up and chat politely with other attendees
2. Tell the group about what you do
3. Listen to what other people do
4. Have one-to-one chats, telling people more about what you do
5. Exchange business cards
6. Listen to a round-up by the organiser, with some pressure about referrals for the next meeting
7. Go home

Some of the people reading this must have much more positive impressions of networking meetings, so apologies if we have just tarnished the concept. Either way, we want to change the whole way you think about networking.

NETWORKING NEVER NEEDS TO FEEL FORCED AND YOU DON'T NEED TO USE UP VALUABLE TIME TO ATTEND EXTRA MEETINGS TO DO IT.

If you work from home or with a restricted number of colleagues, you will have to make the effort to get out and get yourself around other people whenever you can. After that, networking can be something you quickly become comfortable doing all of the time, whatever you are doing. The key thing is that you get used to talking to everyone you meet with the intention of opening up a business connection, which is surprisingly easy to do.

The hugely successful motivational speaker, Les Brown, says you should work with a three-foot rule. If someone comes within three feet of you, find out who they are and tell them what you do for a living. If they don't know you, they aren't going to be able to do business with you.

Picture yourself in a pub, out for dinner, at a business meeting, at an event, on the train – anywhere. You get talking to someone and ask them what they do. You make sure that you really listen to what they have to say, asking more questions, making it clear you are interested in what they are saying. At this point, you've already got that person on side – everyone loves to talk about what they do to someone who is interested in them. While they're talking, you also keep thinking about how that person's business could relate to yours. You'll be making connections in your mind, thinking of new ways your product or service could become indispensable to them (we hope this is sounding familiar). Because you have already taken time to find out about them, it will be easy to create a link to you and your business, something that will make them interested in staying in contact with you. You might have business contacts that relate to their business. You might even already be able to tell them about your product or service as something they would really like to have. You could give them an experience (we'll tell you how to do that in Chapter 6) and make it easy for them to realise how working with you will benefit them and their company. Before you know it, you've got a solid new contact, a new job or a new client.

It really is that straightforward. Repeat this whenever you meet new people, and very soon you will be in the habit of making new, profitable business connections wherever you go. It won't feel like work or have any of the negative connotations of networking – it will feel like a natural and enjoyable way of generating new work for yourself.

EVERYONE WHO KNOWS LEE KNOWS THAT HE'S A MONSTER NETWORKER – he reckons it's become an addiction. And it's rubbing off on the rest of us. Lee can walk into a room where nobody knows him, but soon everyone will. Whenever he meets someone who he thinks has a link, he arranges a coffee with them. Often, he doesn't even know yet why he's arranged the meeting, and the other person asks the same, but they'll sit down and talk, then suddenly, 'Oh, that's really useful – I didn't know you did that' or 'I know so-and-so', and suddenly Lee's got a new link, a new contact or a new job. Then another one, and another one . . .

Here's an example of how indirect links – links with people and companies that you're not doing business with – have a positive impact. Lee meets lots of photographers in the wedding business. He talks to them about the power of having a magician at an event, how that enhances the photos, which in itself encourages them to sell him to their own clients. They go away telling everyone about what he does, showing them pictures of what it can create. And Lee reciprocates – he uses his own networking to sell that photographer. He tells each photographer about his following on social media, and that if they send him their images and they sell him, he will remember that and offer them a job back. Not only that, but Lee puts the photographer's pictures in an album on his Facebook page, with all their details and their website link. He encourages them to visit his page, to look at the albums for all the photographers there, each with their own profile and details. Then he'll add a sponsored boost on the weekend they send him their pictures, and that will go to Lee's other clients. It's free advertising – what photographer is going to turn down an offer like that? Still, some do decline, but then he doesn't want to do business with them – they don't understand the power of impact networking. But that is very rare, which is why he has so many allies in the wedding industry.

With all the photographers' photos, Lee's Facebook page looks fantastic, with continuously updated content. The photographers go away and tell everyone how great he is, and Lee is the first magician they recommend to their clients. Lee enjoys the same results in the corporate world – through photographers, event planners and venues – because he is so active on social media. He does more on social media for some venues than they do for themselves!

The same applies to social, everyday encounters. Whenever Lee meets someone, instead of just saying 'Oh, nice to meet you, here's a business card', he says 'I tell you what – there's a link between us; I'd love to see you again. I love your work. What are you doing next week? Let's try and arrange a meeting.' If he arranges ten meetings in a month, he knows at least one of them will generate him an income. He asks them all about their business, what they do, how long they've been doing it. They talk and talk and talk; Lee listens and listens and listens. Then he'll say 'Oh, I know someone who's involved with that – they might be able to help you', even if that's not him. It's about having an engaging conversation with people, and then talking about the other things he does, about the things they could do together. Then he meets up with that person and follows through the same process as with the photographers, always making sure there's a benefit to that person, one way or another. It's all about creating a massive network.

This applies to any area of business. It's not only about social media – that's just an example – it's about non-stop networking. EVERY PERSON YOU MEET HAS A LINK. Lee collects business cards wherever he goes –

from clients, venues, suppliers, everyone. He stores standard notes on his phone, things like 'Lovely meeting you today', 'Here are my details', 'Hope we can do business in the future', 'I'd like to find out more about what you do'. Later that day – when he gets home, or while he's still on the train – he fires off an email to every single business address. If someone doesn't reply, he knows he doesn't have the connection with them – they don't have the same interests and/or ambition. But 95% of people do respond – a massive network of likeminded people, each with a link to his business.

MAKE IT BIGGER

It is so incredibly easy to start making new connections, wherever you are and whatever you are doing. VOLUME (networking with everyone), IMPACT (providing an impression or experience that makes you memorable) AND ACTION (doing as much as you can all of the time) will automatically generate work for you. If you can provide an experience that a new connection wants to share with other people, before long you will have created a massive pipeline of new opportunities for your business.

If you make a big enough impression – enough impact – people will keep networking for you long after you have met with them. You don't have to own the room or be the life and soul of the party to make a lasting impression – that can even have a negative effect. People are more likely to be impressed by what you say and what you are offering, as well as your interest in them. And when you do a good job or deliver an excellent product, with good customer service and aftercare, people will keep spreading the word on your behalf.

If you're not sure about how you can be more active, here are just a few examples of how we do it, to inspire you to think about ways you can do the same.

- We might sometimes decide to do magic on a commuter train, in the rush hour, and in no time we've got the full attention of everyone in the carriage. Spencer's picked up a wedding booking just by doing that. Lee leaves his business card anywhere – say, when he's out for dinner, he'll leave his business card on the table at the end of the meal. One day, someone will pick it up, and he'll get an enquiry. There was one time when the magicians Keelan Leyser and Matt Daniel-Baker found his business card on the floor in JFK airport in New York, took a picture of it, and posted it on Facebook. That was before Lee was big on social media – brilliant, free publicity.

- Every magician thinks it's near impossible to get work soon after Christmas, but you only have to take a walk around central London during those months. There's something going on every night of the week all year round, with hundreds of events we would perform for, all in one tiny area in London. It's only about getting on the radar of those event organisers, with massive amounts of action.

- We've both performed for free at times, say if we had the opportunity to be in front of a room full of people that have never met us. Say, if business was slow, we both realised that if we were at home doing nothing, we'd be better off going and doing something at an event and meeting a crowd full of people. We would then have the opportunity to hand out 80–100 business cards, which we otherwise wouldn't be handing out.

- A big part of our business comes from the trade show industry, selling solutions to companies, helping them get their business message delivered. We soon realised we hadn't even touched the surface of the potential market, so we increased our activity by making more phone calls, walking trade show floors, delivering to clients, speaking to people and telling them what we do. Then every now and again, we'd get a bite – a client we otherwise wouldn't have had. Then at that one trade show, everyone sees the value of what you do, and you get another client.

- If we're doing a gig, it's never just a gig in its own right. It's a constant advert for all the following ones. If we perform at a venue, or at a wedding or a wedding fair, we will always go out of our way to speak to the staff at the venue, to establish a meaningful relationship.

- We both make a really big effort to keep following up with previous clients. Everyone loves to feel valued! Even if it's just a quick email to say, 'Are you doing your event again this year?', 'I haven't heard from you recently. How are you? Are you doing anything this year?'. Some of them will say 'No, not this year', but you're still fresher in their mind than you were before you sent the email. Others will come back to you straight away: 'Yes, we are – glad you got in touch – we've got this event coming up . . .'. Then the chances are, we'll pick up more work from that event – the *MAGIC VORTEX*. We're surprised by how many people don't stay in touch with past clients – they're back to coasting. They've had a good year, they relax, then they wonder the following year why they're not as busy. The person you've been dealing with might have left the company, so you need to get on the radar of the person who's replaced them. One minute they've never heard of you, the next they're saying, 'Oh, I didn't know about that – what have you done for us before?' . . . and you're on the way to securing contact.

These are just a few examples, but it all comes down to this: it's about going out there and actually doing something. IF YOU DO NOTHING, NO ONE WILL FIND YOU. You need to keep expanding your network, adding more value and maintaining the relationship, to keep the momentum going.

MAKE IT HAPPEN

We have to quickly re-emphasise here the action part of the equation. You need to make sure you follow up with every single new contact that could benefit your business. Get their card, or at least their contact details, and fire off an email to arrange a meeting with them. Do it the same day, and you will make them feel more important to you, while increasing your importance to them. Arrange an informal chat over coffee to discuss a vague link between your businesses, invite them to an important client meeting, or anything in between. You will be cementing a new relationship and opening new doors. If the other person doesn't reply to your email, let it go – you need to be putting yourself amongst likeminded, positive and proactive people.

MAKE IT DIFFERENT

Imagine you are a plumber. There are three main local outlets where people go to buy their bathroom supplies when they're getting their bathrooms refurbished, which is the ideal type of job for your business. So you make time to visit those outlets now and again, to get to know the salespeople. You show an interest in everything they have to offer and talk to them about their business. Then, when the opportunity arises, you do some free work for them – maybe plumb in an impressive shower, one they make good profit on. You make their display different and interesting, and customers are impressed by seeing the shower in action.

If you are a plumber, please don't laugh at this example – we don't have any knowledge about whether a bathroom shop owner would ever want a functioning shower in their showroom, but that's irrelevant. WHATEVER LINE OF BUSINESS YOU ARE IN, YOU CAN THINK OF A SMALL AMOUNT OF WORK YOU CAN DO FOR A SUPPLIER TO MAKE THEM REMEMBER YOU. And there's a reason why we chose plumbing as an example, which we'll come to in a minute. The point for now is that, whereas last week the bathroom shop had no idea who you were, after one afternoon of working and bantering with the owners and employees, you will now be the first plumber they think of when anyone asks them for a recommendation.

For our work performing at weddings, parties and corporate events, venues are one of the most important sources of recommendation. Our goal is to have every venue know who we are. When they hear the word 'magician' we want the first name that pops into their head to be Spencer Wood or Lee Smith. We go out of our way to visit every single venue within a 100-mile radius, to make sure they know about each of us. We show them what we do, talk about our events and our portfolios, find ways to make sure that we are the people they remember. We send cards, flowers and/or gifts, to thank them for making us feel like a part of their team when performing at the venue. For our highest-valued venues, we offer complimentary magic performances, so that they know what they're offering to their top clients.

Here's the reason we used plumbing as an example earlier. When we were researching for this book and talking on this subject, a friend of ours gave us a counter-example. She had visited a bathroom shop looking for a new bathroom suite, the salesperson asked her which plumber she was using, but he didn't recognise the name of the plumber. Even though the plumber had been recommended, our friend now started to have doubts about how reliable and established he was. She stayed with the plumber and was happy with everything he did, but she swears she would have been happier from the start and more likely to recommend the plumber to friends if the bathroom salesperson had reacted positively when he'd heard his name.

MAKE EVERYONE MATTER

Whatever business you are in, you have to realise that NETWORKING ISN'T ONLY ABOUT CHARMING PROSPECTS AND INCREASING YOUR CLIENT BASE. As we've just illustrated, a good relationship with suppliers can be very rewarding, but the same goes for just about anybody you come into contact with. In addition to bathroom suppliers, a plumber will benefit from recommendations from hardware stores, kitchen showrooms, gas engineers, architects, builders, home-extension teams and housing developers. Then anyone in a public-facing role, say a pub landlord or a hairdresser, has daily conversations with people who are likely to ask for a recommendation for a plumber. We thought of those within five minutes of considering trades related to an industry we've never worked in. Whatever industry you are in, keep making time to think about all the people who could generate work for you, even if the link isn't immediately obvious, then make time to create a positive impression with those people.

We have both had a great time over the last few years, helping businesses to maximise their presence at trade shows. You've no doubt been to trade shows and seen some poor employees there, looking hopeful as you walk past their stand, while you try to avoid eye contact. That's the opposite of any stand we have worked on. We've developed the skills to draw in crowds and ensure everyone leaves buzzing, with a lasting and positive impression of the company and products we're representing. And we're not talking about only the normal trade show visitors. We've worked for corporate clients in the trade show industry who've said things like, 'Don't bother talking to those people – they're just installers'. But every single person at the trade show is in some way connected to the same industry. Even if a person doesn't seem to be important, as in they're not a prospective client, if you establish a valuable connection they will go away and tell other (important) people about what you do.

DON'T CREATE NEGATIVITY BY DECIDING THAT ANYONE ISN'T IMPORTANT TO YOU. Every single person needs to know who you are, and it doesn't matter how they find out. A huge amount of our work comes from people we wouldn't normally work with, who have gone away and told other people about us. That comes from the amount of noise we make, with anyone we meet. The same should apply to every single business, every single industry, every single person out there. If someone walks into your car showroom to look at a Ferrari or a Lamborghini, even if they look scruffy or broke, you need to talk to them in just the same way you would talk to someone who looks like they are about to buy a car from you. Both types of people are equally as likely to go away and tell other people about what their experience was like with your company. If you are speaking to someone you know can't buy from you, they will still know someone else who can.

We both have direct experience of how this works. Talking to someone in an airport, who turns out to know a major events organiser. Doing a card trick for someone on a train, whose friend runs a company organising Asian weddings. The list is endless. Start connecting with anyone and everyone, and you will start to experience significant changes to your business.

At one of his first meetings with Trevor Liley, Trevor said to Lee, 'See that person over there? That person will never book you.'

'Why?'

'Because he doesn't know who you are. You need every single person on the planet to know who you are, then you will never be out of work. The more people who know who you are, the more work you're going to get.'

There are plenty of other ways to do marketing. We both get great business revenue from Facebook, for example; we'll come back to the power of social media in Chapter 8. But if someone has seen one of our adverts on Facebook, they might be inspired but then search the internet and choose someone else.

Business is and always will be about people, and there is no stronger way of making powerful and rewarding connections than face to face, by making a positive impression on someone you have met in person. PRACTISE NON-STOP NETWORKING UNTIL IT BECOMES SECOND NATURE. Work hard at increasing your volume, the number of people you reach, and keeping in touch with everyone you can. Go the extra mile for your most important connections, but never underestimate the power of a recommendation from just about anyone.

CHAPTER 5
Infinite connectivity

We're going to invite you to relax for a bit. Get yourself a cup of coffee or a glass of wine and put your feet up. The last few chapters have delivered a load of new ideas on mentality and action, and you're really going to have to pay attention when you're reading the chapters that follow this one. So, take some time out now and enjoy some upbeat encouragement, while we tell you about the benefits of improving your connectivity.

Networking is so closely related to connectivity that the difference between them might not be obvious. Here's the distinction: networking is about putting yourself out there, getting in front of as many people as you can. Connectivity is about finding ways to get amongst the right people, for specific reasons. It's about focusing long-term on connecting with the people who are going to have the biggest influences on you and make significant differences to the development of your business. In this chapter we will talk about WHO it's best to connect with, HOW you can go about it and WHY you need to improve your connectivity. Then we'll talk about doing it all BACKWARDS.

There are two reasons we have added the word 'infinite' to the title of this chapter. Like non-stop networking, connectivity is something you have to work at all of the time. Again, it will soon become second nature, and the rewards far outweigh the effort you put in. At the end of this chapter, you will also find out about making yourself memorable. Okay, so no one's going to remember you for infinity, but you need to make sure you stick in anyone's mind for as long as they can help you to develop your business ... and to create further powerful connections.

WHO

Even if you don't know much about a new acquaintance, there are ways of judging pretty quickly how successful they are. Not based on material objects – if they drive a good car, they might still be up to their eyeballs in debt. But if, for example, you meet a businessperson who talks in time – when you arrange a meeting and they say 'OK, I can do 20 minutes' – you can be 99% sure they are busy because they are successful. Or vice versa, that they are successful because they manage their time carefully. People who don't cap the time they spend on something won't generally be worth spending time with.

OTHER SIGNS THAT CAN INDICATE SOMEONE IS DRIVEN AND SUCCESSFUL:

- They crave knowledge, including showing interest in you and your business
- They are confident enough to share their own knowledge and business ideas
- They're organised and happy to plan ahead
- They are self-assured and assertive, without being arrogant or overbearing
- They don't waste time complaining, instead looking for the positive side of any situation

When you meet someone with all those characteristics, you are just about guaranteed to benefit from connecting and developing a relationship with them.

On the other hand, you might already know about a good number of successful people, in your line of business or in your local area. Nine times out of ten, it will be worth putting in the extra effort to make a connection with them and develop those relationships. However, don't be afraid of re-evaluating any new relationship you establish. No matter how successful someone is, if they turn out to be self-interested and negative, you need to tactfully cut them loose.

HOW

So, you have accepted that it will benefit you and your business to develop relationships with successful people, but how do you go about making those connections in the first place? One of the key factors here is taking everything up a level. If you are used to dealing with the account managers at a company you work with, make a massive effort to get in contact with their MANAGER OR ANOTHER KEY DECISION MAKER. If you are approaching a new client, instead of arranging a meeting with the salespeople, make a conscious decision to meet with the managing director. It will be harder – it might take you a month to set up a meeting – but it will be worth it. Once you have got through to the key decision maker, you will be in the position to sign a bigger contract immediately, rather than waiting for salespeople to pass your details on without communicating any of the energy and dedication that you present yourself with. You will only get further up the ladder by raising your profile and making the right connections. We can *categorically* say that all of the major contracts we have worked on have come from meetings with the people higher up in the respective companies, people who have the authority to make bigger decisions.

What if you are looking to establish entirely new connections, with people and companies you haven't yet worked with? To make you realise how easy that can be, we're going to shrink the world a bit first.

There is a well-established theory, called the 'six degrees of separation', which claims that any two people in the world can be connected via six links. This isn't about finding out about other people, which takes only seconds on social media – it's about linking two different people via six mutual connections, through friends and acquaintances. It's even been tested, by sending parcels from one person, across six mutual connections, to reach someone in a completely different area and social environment. There are around 7.5 billion people on this planet.

Even if the real number of mutual acquaintances linking any two people is seven or eight, how small does it make the world feel? And it's likely that you could connect to anyone in (or related to) your line of work via only two or three other connections. Someone you already know will know someone else, who knows the person that could make a massive difference to you.

It's incredibly easy now to find out who is most successful in an area you would most like to work in. Once you have identified a contact you would benefit from knowing, find out who knows them, then work it back to someone you already know. Without too much effort, you will then be able to develop relationships to engineer a get-together with the person at the top of the tree. Do some research before you meet them, to find out about their interests and their business, and it won't be long before you have developed a powerful new connection.

WHY

Human beings are social animals. We mix together, live together and learn together. We depend on social interaction so intensely that solitary confinement has devastating effects on the unfortunate minority of people who experience it. SOCIAL INTERACTION IS VITALLY FULFILLING. We 100% need to be around other people and to be accepted by them. And the types of people you spend the most time with make a vital difference to your own behaviour and outcomes.

For example, if you hang around with people who joke about how unfit they are, eat junk food and go out drinking most weekends, it's pretty unlikely that you're going to become a health and fitness fanatic. But if your closest friends regularly go to the gym, follow healthy diets and are more likely to be on a spa break than down the pub at the weekend, it's almost inevitable that you will be motivated to adopt the same mindset, setting yourself higher health and fitness goals.

Exactly the same principles apply in business. THE MORE YOU HANG OUT WITH HIGH-ACHIEVING FRIENDS AND BUSINESS CONTACTS, THE MORE MOTIVATED YOU WILL BE TO ACHIEVE MORE. The more business ideas you share with likeminded, positive people, the more they will share with you. If you've been charging £100 for a service you provide, then you start mixing with people who do the same for £200, there's no doubt you will feel the need *and* the confidence to charge more. If you establish a new set of business associates, all of whom set themselves high monthly and annual targets, you will suddenly feel you ought to be doing the same (and before long you'll wonder how you ever got by without doing it). And successful people will support you, reacting positively to anything new you achieve, encouraging you to achieve even more. There is nothing to lose.

Now, you don't have to ditch all your mates and become a pretentious idiot. But as soon as you start making more conscious decisions about who you spend time with, you will begin to notice a difference. Invest more time with the people you already know who are more outgoing and driven. Prioritise any new relationships you develop with people who are successful and positive. Make a real effort to engage with people who are achieving a higher level of success than you, in any area of business, and you will experience improvements in your own motivation and success levels.

THE BBT – Business Backwards Tree

Through our daily talks and mind-mapping meetings, we have developed a new way of strengthening the power of connectivity: by working backwards down the chain of connections that got us to a successful person or job. We call it the BBT, THE BUSINESS BACKWARDS TREE.

If you are still only in the planning stages of setting up your own business, make a clear mental note to come back to this section later. If you've been running your own business for a year or more, you will almost certainly be able to think now of your three key clients – the people or companies that have contributed the most to the income and success of your business. You will probably also be able to instantly name the three most important jobs, assignments or contracts – the ones that have brought you the biggest financial income and/or business opportunities.

Now we want you to spend some time working out how you got to your key clients and to your most successful jobs. Make a list, going back as far as you can. You'll be able to work out a CLEAR ROUTE, in a series of steps, showing how you got to the final key client or contract. Do the same for your other key clients and jobs, and you might well start to see a repeating pattern, a successful route that it is worth focusing on replicating in order to make other powerful connections. Even if there is no pattern between the three different clients or jobs, you will still have a much clearer picture in your mind about the types of people and situations that helped you to make the most profitable connections.

Here's an example of a job we both recently worked on, one that earned us more than any other job we had previously done. We spent four days in Dubai, all expenses paid, then received a very generous payment for just 90 seconds of performing on stage. It was, essentially, a life-changing job. Now we've looked carefully at how we got there. It all started through a few influential people we met in the UK, who took us through to high-end corporate jobs. Because of the people who worked for those clients, our profile had a massive boost, leading to the key person in Saudi Arabia hearing about us and making enquiries. At the time of writing, we're working on re-engineering that whole process.

You can take it a level further back: we first met the influential people in the UK by working with smaller corporate clients, which brings us full circle to the start of this chapter, to the infinite power of connectivity. Whoever you are dealing with now, don't coast – keep working at developing new relationships and establishing more powerful connections, and you'll be amazed by the results.

While we're on the subject of key clients, we have to emphasise the importance of nurturing your most important connections at all times. It is absolutely vital that you DON'T EVER TAKE POWERFUL CONNECTIONS FOR GRANTED – even a business associate who has become a friend, or a company that has been happy to do business with you for years, can disappear as soon as someone else makes a bigger or better impression.

You need to focus on the relationships with all your key clients, maintaining regular contact and making extra effort to ensure they feel appreciated, for example taking them out to dinner or giving them exclusive offers. IT IS JUST AS IMPORTANT TO MAINTAIN AND STRENGTHEN EXISTING CONNECTIONS AS IT IS TO DEVELOP NEW ONES.

BE MEMORABLE

It's not going to be much use to you if you set up a new contact, the other person likes you and what you have to say, but then a week later they can hardly remember you.

Lee reckons that one of the best things Trevor Liley ever did for him, at one of their first meetings, was to annihilate him. Lee had gone into the meeting feeling very self-assured – he was successful as a magician, all the magicians on the circuit knew him, and he was earning a good salary. Lee was now planning to develop his trade show presence and was looking forward to meeting up with Trevor, to establish more contacts and even to take on some of his work. Trevor tore Lee to pieces in under 30 seconds.

THE CONVERSATION WENT SOMETHING LIKE THIS:

'Lee, what do you do?'

'What do you mean?'

'What do you do?'

'I do magic.'

'So? What do you do? I've got some money in my pocket, I might want to book you. What do you do?'

'What?'

'What do you mean, "What?"? What do you DO?'

Lee was completely thrown. He said, 'I do tricks.'

'But what do you do? Why would I want to book you, if you don't even know what you do? Ask me what I do.'

'Er . . . what do you do?'

'My name's Trevor Liley, I run a very successful business company called TLP. I make companies hundreds of thousands of pounds. I give them a massive return on investment because they can't do it. That's what I do. Now, what do you do?'

Eventually, Trevor said, 'Do it again – you need to get this. Pretend I'm you, do it again'.

Lee asked Trevor what he did. Trevor replied, 'My name's Lee Smith. I'm a magician, but forget that. What I will do is create an experience for your event, an experience so powerful that people remember me and your event for ever. Not only that, if you book me, you'll get the credit for that experience.'

Lee started applying this approach at wedding fairs, and his wedding business tripled.

WHATEVER YOU ARE DOING, YOU NEED TO WORK ON YOUR OPENING LINE, the one that creates with most powerful impact about what you are going to give the person you are talking to, how you are going to make their life better. You will learn more about how to do this – how to create your WIDIFY – in the next chapter. For now, you need to focus on creating an instant emotional connection, on promising to deliver something, so that the person you are talking to will immediately want to engage further with you. Something they want to find out more about, which will make sure they want (or need) to stay in contact with you. Then you will have a powerful new connection.

This chapter has told you how to improve your connectivity and given you ideas on the most important people you need to connect with. We've explained how to make new connections and how to be remembered. There are plenty of other ways you can and need to make yourself memorable, but they relate to further down the line, including creating a demand for what you do, delivering with impact and developing successful sales strategies. That's where we're going next.

CHAPTER 6

Selling made easy

The middle chapter, and core to your business success: selling. It's the part most people seem to feel especially uncomfortable about, but however brilliant your product or service is, there's no way to avoid selling if you want to be successful.

Virtual and digital marketing can be vital for raising brand awareness and getting your product to market, but face-to-face marketing is the most effective way to build customer loyalty, increase sales and improve retention levels. Even if you are using other companies' platforms – selling via wholesalers, distributors or retailers – you still need to connect with the right people to get your product into those distribution channels. As we illustrated in Chapter 4, business revolves around people. If you can make a strong connection with someone and deliver them a solution, you are virtually guaranteed to close the sale.

In this chapter, we will teach you the fundamental principles of how to improve your sales techniques, to maximise your success in getting your product or service to market. We're also going to make you realise that SELLING IS MUCH EASIER AND MORE ENJOYABLE THAN YOU PROBABLY THINK IT IS.

WIFM – WHAT'S IN IT FOR ME?

We can't guess how many books and blogs have been written on this subject, but we're going to give you a condensed version – an easy overview of how you can immediately start to improve your sales technique. In short: any prospect or client only wants to know what's in it for them.

You will have found a gap in the market and feel that other people will benefit from buying what you offer. You know all about your product or service, about how brilliant it is and why you have designed it the way it is. You could talk for an hour about all the facts, features and figures . . . but people don't want to hear about all that. Before anyone has decided to buy a product or service, they are only ever going to be interested in whether and how it is going to improve their life. Take a look around any room. We promise you that every single manufactured product you see will deliver at least one benefit and/or solution. And it was bought because the purchaser thought that the product would improve their life.

Before you even think about going to your next sales meeting, making a call to a prospect or telling anyone about what you do, you need to do some research to work out exactly how you or your product can improve someone's life. Not only what *anyone* might gain from the product, but the reasons it is right for a SPECIFIC CLIENT OR YOUR TARGET CUSTOMER. In Chapter 10, we'll give you an extra tool to help you judge the type and character of anyone you're dealing with. For now, we're talking purely about researching all the background details and facts you can, in order to learn about what is most important to your prospect. You're probably only going to have one opportunity with this client, and there is no point telling them, say, all about the environmental benefits of using your product, then realising they don't even believe in global warming. The more you can find out in advance about your target customer or a specific client, the more successful you will be in selling them your product.

Make notes – on your PC or on a sheet of paper – with two columns: FACT/FEATURE and BENEFIT/WIFM. In the first column, write down every detail you can think of about your product or service. In the second column, explain how each detail could improve another person's life. You need to keep asking yourself here 'so what?', until you get to all the crucial underlying benefits.

For example:

This hybrid car is environmentally friendly and more efficient than the one you drive now.

So what?

It produces lower emissions and uses less fuel.

So what?

It's better for your health and costs less to run.

So what?

You will feel better and you'll have extra money to put towards your next holiday.

It's not that people aren't intelligent enough to work out the link between the first and the last statements about the car, but it's human nature not to automatically make the link. The prospect probably already knows they should be bothered about the environment and trying to save money, but it's only when you translate that into personal benefits to them – that they will feel better and be closer to affording their holiday – that they will have a personal interest in buying your hybrid car.

Let's take a really basic example of a WIFM list, based around what we do for our trade show clients. Trade shows can give great returns, through brand awareness, on-site sales and establishing new leads. But they are a substantial financial investment for any company, and it can be extremely hard to get noticed at a huge trade show, with all the other businesses vying for attention. Even the most successful sales staff might not have experience in selling face to face in this type of environment. And however many people notice your stand, it is very difficult to guarantee any ongoing connection with them. So our WIFM model could look like this:

FACT/FEATURE (what we do)	**BENEFIT/WIFM** (what's in it for the client)
Brilliant, unique entertainment by a professional who is very experienced in drawing in crowds, maximising footfall to your stand	Confidence that my company will stand out from others at the show; my boss will think I'm great for finding and booking this person
Engaging with your prospects on an emotional level, making them laugh and tell others about your company	Positive, engaging impression of my business, with increased company and brand awareness – exactly what we need from this show
Many years of experience in face-to-face sales, with high success rates	Qualified leads who will place orders on the day and/or engage with us on an ongoing basis
Highly effective sales training, to prepare your staff members before the show and enable them to achieve new levels of success at this and future trade shows	What a relief, not having to stress about preparing my sales team. This has got to be an incredibly good investment . . .
Guaranteed return on investment . . .	. . . at last, ROI on a trade show. The CEO is going to be seriously impressed if I make this happen.

Of course, by now the company is already on board – we have told them everything they wanted to hear and presented ourselves as the ideal trade show solution. Look back at the columns and you will see that magic – our passion and what we love doing to entertain people – hasn't featured once on that list. **This is all about what is in it for them.**

WIDIFY – WHY I DO IT FOR YOU

A few months before publishing this book, we realised what was missing from the standard WIFM principle. It's been phenomenal for both of us since then, seeing other people's reactions when they understand our new WIDIFY process and work out how they can apply it to their business. This is by far the most important section about selling and the foundation for the rest of this chapter. It is not the easiest concept to understand and adapt to your product or service, but once you get there, you will never look back.

WIDIFY TAKES WIFM A WHOLE STAGE FURTHER. You will still be applying everything about WIFM, scrutinising your product or service and turning the facts and features into benefits, based on what is most important to your target customer. Now you need to work out how you can build in three extra ingredients: PASSION, EMOTION AND TRUST – YOUR PET – to make it 100% clear to your target customer why you are doing it for them – your WIDIFY.

PASSION gives you the first part of your WIDIFY: 'why I do it'. Passion is contagious. If you believe in your product and are genuine, engaged and enthusiastic whenever you talk about it, you'll overpower any negativity or doubt in the room.

If you have any doubt about how much passion you radiate, take time to work out why you are doing what you do. Don't feel bad if your first response is that you are running your business to earn money – that's the first thing most people think of. Just dig deeper. You could be in any line of business, but why have you chosen yours? Why do you love doing what you do? What makes you sure that people will enjoy the improvements to their life if they use your product or service? This isn't about working out what you want to achieve in the future and how to get there – you need to look in the opposite direction, at your own values and beliefs, about what has got you to where you are now. Think back to the times when you've had the best responses and reactions from your previous clients, what those clients were saying and how they were reacting, to remind you of exactly what future clients will experience. A fellow magician, BEN FIELD, who attended our first STEP System

Seminar, gave a great example: 'I was thinking back to one of my first professional gigs, it was the third or fourth paid gig I did; it was unusual as it was a kids' birthday party with mostly adults there. I remember doing the kids' magic show and then busting out the balloons, and ending up with a queue of adults wanting all sorts of crazy balloons. One of the kids just pulled up a chair and sat and watched me for the rest of the party, and all the adults were telling me how amazing I was. I left that party welling up with pride, knowing that I had made a lasting memory for both the kids and the adults . . . Sometimes we undervalue our WIDIFY because it can become common to us as we do it all the time, so if you're struggling to come up with something, think back to your early career and remember when you truly realised the impact you had on other people.'

Keep thinking of all the benefits and solutions that you can deliver, and you will suddenly find that you have developed a genuine passion for what you do. That passion will instantly give you a stronger connection with anyone you talk to about your product or service.

EMOTION is crucial to the WIDIFY equation. If you can ENGAGE WITH YOUR PROSPECT ON AN EMOTIONAL LEVEL, you will increase your chances of developing a strong and long-lasting relationship, as well as making them considerably more likely to want to buy from you. Here's a list of the most powerful emotions, including a basic example on how each emotion could be used within a sales pitch.

HAPPINESS – What a beautiful place to be, everyone still talking about your wedding six months later.

CURIOSITY – Wouldn't you love to know how easy it is to . . . ?

INCLUSION – It's going to be great for you, being part of the growing number of people who . . .

PRIDE – Imagine your friends' reactions.

ANGER – Do you ever feel let down, knowing that . . . ?

EXCITEMENT – This is a once-in-a-lifetime opportunity for you.

CONFIDENCE – These will make you feel invincible.

SADNESS – Just £5 per month from you will help dogs like Archie to get better.

ANXIETY – Don't you just hate the feeling when . . . ?

DISGUST – What if you were stuck somewhere, with no access to clean drinking water?

EMBARRASSMENT – There's nothing worse than when you . . .

FEAR – Imagine how you'd feel if all your guests were bored.

SURPRISE – You'll be amazed by how quickly you can . . .

JEALOUSY – Your colleagues will be envious!

CALM – You can forget about all the stress and time it takes to . . .

GUILT – It's awful when you know you're not spending enough time with your kids.

After you have researched your ideal customer to find out what is most important to them, it will be easy to link more powerful emotions to your product or service, to trigger emotional connections.

Look back at the list above, and you will notice that one word is common to each statement: YOU. Place emphasis whenever you can on engaging with your prospect's emotions, rather than how other people may feel. It can help to give examples of other clients who already use your product – a strong testimonial is one of the most powerful marketing tools. But always bring it back round to 'you', highlighting how your prospect could enjoy the same positive outcome. Couple that approach with a strong emotional connection, and you will have only one more factor missing from your WIDIFY equation . . .

TRUST is the most important factor in any business relationship. When a company is offering something we want, as long as we trust and believe in them, we will be 100% WILLING TO BUY THAT PRODUCT from them.

There are many ways you can build trust with your prospects and clients, in addition to making emotional connections. We'll start with a quick list, to remind you of things that might seem obvious but are easy to forget when you're in a meeting. Then we'll get on to the main point that we think gets overlooked.

Demonstrate credibility – practise delivering confidently and authoritatively, and give examples of satisfied customers, including testimonials and personal stories

Value their time – be punctual, respond promptly to calls and emails, and stick to any deadlines you arrange (or keep your prospect updated if there are unavoidable delays)

Respect their views – don't disregard their opinions, and show concern for any problems they have experienced, especially any that relate to previous providers

Be yourself – be genuine and friendly, and don't be afraid to admit if you can't immediately answer a question (then don't forget to follow up with them later)

Ask questions and listen – don't start off with a prepared script; it's much better to ask your prospect first about what's important to them

Before you next meet with a prospect or existing client, we want you to do some homework to determine your core beliefs in the value of your product or service. Write down every single positive feature, benefit and detail about what you deliver, and think of every single positive solution it could provide. Think outside the box and add everything else that comes to light. Google every single problem related to what you do, then identify the ways that your product or service delivers solutions. Dig deeper again, create mind maps, talk it through with clients, friends and peers – whatever you need to do to define the true values of your product or service.

Everyone knows if a salesperson is embellishing facts around their product or just saying what they think someone wants to hear. But if you already know and truly believe in all the benefits and solutions you're offering, your prospect will develop a strong and lasting trust in you and your company.

WHEN YOU HAVE COMPLETED ALL THIS BACKGROUND WORK, IT IS LIKELY YOU WILL HAVE THE EUREKA WIDIFY MOMENT. You'll have identified a genuine passion for your product or service. You'll have found ways to make an emotional connection with your prospects, to make them want to buy from you. You won't just be talking about yourself, you'll be telling your prospect what's in it for them and how they can trust you – why you are doing it for *them*. And it will be hard not to convert any sale.

WIDIFY isn't only for face-to-face sales pitches – you can now start to live and breathe your values and beliefs, building them into every part of your marketing. You will feel a whole new level of trust emanating from anyone you talk to about your product, making it infinitely more likely that they will go away and tell other people about you.

Once you have conquered the whole of WIDIFY, don't forget to keep your PET with you at all times, and you will start to see massive improvements. The rest of this chapter gives additional tips to help you polish your pitch.

WhySPs

You'll no doubt have already heard the standard business-development advice, based on a concept invented in the 1940s, that every company needs to identify a USP, a unique selling point. We are still told we need to find something that makes our product or service completely different from all the others. But nearly all the business owners we've worked with have admitted they find this advice intimidating or restrictive. There are lots of small things they do differently, but they can't identify one outstanding point that makes them completely different from and better than every other company in the market. We want to UPDATE THIS CONCEPT, to make it a lot easier and much more powerful.

After all, even if you can identify one thing that makes your business different, that single point isn't going to be valuable to all your prospective clients. We want you to think more flexibly, to keep identifying all the selling points that make you and your product or service stand out, then to keep emphasising the most important points at different times, depending on the situation and the person you are talking to. These are client-specific selling points that highlight why they will benefit from buying from you more than from other companies. We call them WhySPs (PRONOUNCED 'Y-S-Ps').

When you've completed the background work around WIFM and WIDIFY, you will have established the key values of your target customer. You can then emphasise in all your marketing why you and your company are different from others and better at meeting those key values and solving potential pain points. For example, if most of your clients are busy or stressed, illustrate the reasons your specific product or service will save them time. If you are targeting higher-end customers, place the strongest emphasis on the quality of your product, compared with others, and how it will reflect their own image, including recommendations for your company from other high-end clients. If you want to partner with a company that is relatively new to market, highlight all the ways that you will be able to increase their market presence better than other companies. There just doesn't need to be a limit to the selling points – emphasise particular WhySPs in your different campaigns, marketing areas and lines of communication.

If you are offering a product that essentially doesn't differ from others on the market, or something people will choose according to their personal taste, look for the WhySPs about *you*. After all, business is all about people buying from other people – MORE OFTEN THAN NOT IT'S THE PERSON THAT PEOPLE BUY INTO, NOT THE PRODUCT. Think outside the box and find the thing that makes you different, to demonstrate why buying from you will provide a positive experience. Anything from your presence on social media, for example, to your exceptional sales aftercare, will make you more attractive to your prospect.

Please don't forget to make your WhySPs about what the other person really wants, not about what is personally most important to you. Then it is very likely that another **MAGIC VORTEX** will evolve – the results you see from highlighting your WhySPs will help you to develop your product, to make it even more successful with your target audience.

Our copy-editor, Ilsa Hawtin, helped us to define and develop the WhySPs concept, based on her own experiences. At the end of this chapter, you will find her examples of how it works for her business.

LOSE THE FEAR OF SELLING

There's something about selling that makes it feel a really negative prospect to most people, which leads to the statement you hear so often: 'I hate selling'. It's probably mainly from personal experience – you feel a negative and defensive reaction when talking to a cold-caller who's trying to sell you insurance, or anyone who's trying to make you buy something you don't want. If this is reminding you of how uncomfortable you feel about selling your product, we need to help you over that hurdle. You are not going to be doing any persuading, and you are not going to be selling something the other person doesn't want. Don't think of selling as *pushing* – change your mindset to see it as *pulling*. Pulling in the direction of where your prospect needs and wants to go – you only need to take them by the hand and lead. If you believe in your product and know that it will benefit other people, all you need to do is communicate with them to let them know about your product, and they will want to buy it.

Then there's the second potential hurdle: 'I'm not a salesperson'. BELIEVE US WHEN WE SAY THAT EVERY SINGLE PERSON ON THE PLANET IS A SALESPERSON. It's something we all do, at least in some small way, just about every single day. We bet you anything that the last time you went for a job interview, you didn't think of it as a sales pitch . . . but what else could it be? You went there to communicate the reasons why you thought you were the best person for the job. Before the interview, you tried to think of ways to make yourself stand out from the other candidates – qualities that would appeal to the interviewer, and the ways the company would benefit from employing you. It was a sales pitch.

Ask anyone what they do for a living, and they will sell themselves to you. The conversation could go like this:

'What do you do?'

'I'm a window cleaner.'

'How long have you been doing that?'

'Five years. I like being my own boss, and the money's good, as long as you keep looking for new business. I don't have the overheads of an office or a shop, and I didn't even lose much business in the recession.'

'Where do you work?'

'I cover the south of town – there's easier access to the properties, and the residents are reliable payers.'

'Oh, okay. And what methods do you use, to clean windows?'

'I use the reach-and-wash system, with de-ionised water.'

'Why's that?'

'It's quicker for me and better, because the water doesn't leave any residue. It's also much easier to reach the upper levels – I don't even need a ladder most of the time.'

The window cleaner has just sold you the benefits of his job, the reasons he works where he does and the advantages of using his own method. He wasn't even trying to get you to buy something; he was just putting a positive slant on his explanation. Even if he'd put a negative slant on everything, moaning to you about all the drawbacks, he would have been selling the reasons for why he hates his job.

There are plenty of times every day when you sell in some way, even though you're not consciously aware of it. When you encourage your partner to book a holiday. When you persuade your children to behave differently or to revise for their exams. When you ask someone for a favour, or when you recommend another company to a friend. You're not doing anything devious or underhand, you are purely influencing other people, usually for their own benefit. **Hey, even when you're telling someone you're no good at sales, you are selling them that idea by telling them all the reasons why you believe you can't sell.**

The sooner you get used to the idea that you *are* a salesperson and that there is nothing wrong with selling, the more successful you'll be. Allow yourself to *enjoy* talking about your product, and you will lose any fear you have about selling.

PAIN RELIEF

We've touched on this already in this chapter, but you need to be sure you have a thorough understanding of pain points and how to overcome them. Every single person has things that bug them – things that are unsatisfactory in their life, including the products or services they are already using. When you can identify a person's pain points, you will be in the position to give them a solution, and they will want to buy from you. IT REALLY IS THAT SIMPLE.

When Trevor Liley was teaching Lee about this, he wrote a script for him to take to a meeting with a new company. Lee had already been to a few meetings with Trevor, who now told him, 'Ask these questions, say these things, then watch what happens. I can't tell you any more – just do it'. Lee thought it was never going to work. But he went to the meeting and asked the questions, working his way through the script he had practised, determining the client's pain points. Then he said, 'Here's what I think the solution is . . .', and the client immediately said, 'I'm sold, where do we sign?' Lee had given him a solution.

Here's an example of an area we decided to move into a few years before writing this book. It's the key event for any company that has made a significant investment in terms of time, money and manpower in developing a new product: their product launch. The client wants to raise brand and company awareness, and for the event and product to make a big impression and be memorable for all the VIPs, including their CEO, the press and their top clients. When we're pitching to them, we're going to need to make them value our services over those of any other host or infotainer. Magic will be a small part of what we do at the event, but that's of no interest to the client at this point – they won't see magic as a solution to any potential pain points, and it's likely they can't yet picture how it would relate to their product.

OUR PITCH WOULD GO SOMETHING LIKE THIS:

'Let's think first about the last launch you attended, run by another company. It's likely you enjoyed the canapés and listened to the presentations, all the time wondering how early you could make an excuse to leave. I bet you hardly even remember the product they were launching. Not a bad evening, but not achieving the main goal of the launch, to raise impactful and long-lasting awareness of the product.

'You are now arranging exactly the same type of event, which is going to cost your company £XYZ, and could have the same lack of impact. Imagine now that yours will be completely different. There's a buzz in the air right from the start, then two hours later, no one's looking at their watch. You eavesdrop on some conversations and it's not just small-talk – everyone's talking about your product and when it's going to be available. They're having a laugh and exchanging business cards ... and the global CEO looks like the cat that's got the cream. WE WILL MAKE THAT HAPPEN.

'We want your product launch to be an outstanding success. We will deliver a unique and compelling presentation, created exclusively around your product. We'll deliver with unforgettable impact, so EVERYONE will know what your product is and the solution it provides. We guarantee that everyone will be focused on your company and your new product, for the entire event. Your product launch will be the one that everyone remembers, leading to great press reviews and qualified leads, and giving you a much bigger return on investment. 'This isn't only about the presentations – we'll be there from the start, breaking the ice and getting everyone in a good mood. We'll make sure the atmosphere is right when it comes to the speech by your CEO. You don't need to worry about introducing the presentations – we'll do that for you, making sure everyone is FULLYENGAGED. It's very likely there will be some delays, but we'll fill the gaps and keep everyone entertained. You won't even need to worry if the event overruns – we'll take care of all your guests until the evening is completely over. You can just relax and look forward to positive responses from your colleagues AND the long-lasting impact on your product and your company. We are the complete solution for your product launch.'

We've now highlighted the pain points and delivered the solution. Not only that, but we're coming from a place of authority – we've already ensured the success of a number of other product launches. You can add value, something like: 'If you were to book us for £X to inform and entertain, and book a host separately, for £Y, it would cost you more than just booking us. With two different hosts, you won't have the same continuity, and the other person isn't going to guarantee the same return on investment.'

It's suddenly very unlikely that they're not going to sign up for what we are offering – we have become the product-launch solution they now know they need. But if there's any hesitation: 'You don't even need to book with us today, but you're still going to remember this meeting more than any of the others you've arranged. And you're going to be telling your colleagues about it.' Just saying that, with confidence, makes it happen – you've planted the seed for them to go away and think and talk about you. Then, 'Imagine what your guests are going to experience and how pleased your boss will be. You'll get all the credit for that, for booking us.' Even one simple line like that that can make the difference between them walking away or making a booking.

Now we can say, 'Let's just go over that again, very quickly reiterate. So, do you want to go for only the opening presentation, or the whole evening?'. Now you're backtracking and they're PANICKING, thinking 'What about the product launch – how can I make that the best bit of the evening?'. Nine times out of ten, we'll get the booking for the whole event. They came to the meeting wondering if we'd be the best infotainer for their product launch. Now they HAVE to have us, to cover the whole event – what we're offering has become an essential.

Once you have identified the pain points and worked out a solution, build those into the WIDIFY principle. Focus your WHY I DO IT around your passion for doing what you do. Highlight any potential pain points, then build emotion and trust into the FORYOU solution. If you have made them want your product enough, making the solution to any pain points outweigh the costs, then they will invest in you, every single time.

MAKE A PROMISE

One of the most powerful steps in ensuring a sale is to make a promise about what your product or service will deliver.

Picture this. You have researched carefully and found the ways that your product or service is going to improve someone's life. You have refined your technique of talking with passion about what you do. You highlight all the pain points it's going to relieve for your prospect, and the WhySPs for why they should choose your company over all the others. Not only that, but you have perfected an impactful, personal experience in the way you deliver your sales pitch. Then your prospect asks how certain they can be that the product will work for them . . . and you say 'Well, it should do' or 'It works for most people' or 'I've only had a few people who have been disappointed'. Crash.

DON'T WAIT UNTIL SOMEONE ASKS FOR YOUR PROMISE – SHOUT ABOUT IT ON YOUR MARKETING AND IN YOUR EMAILS. Plaster it all over your website. You can mention it at the beginning of your pitch, then repeat it whenever you feel there's any doubt in the room. When you feel your pitch has probably worked, make your promise again to get them to sign up.

In case you're not sure yet what you should be promising, here are some examples:

Lose half a stone within six months!

The most comfortable shoes you'll ever wear

Stress-free time management

The ideal cost-saving app

How to get a better night's sleep

When you think about applying a promise to what you offer, you might feel nervous about promising satisfaction. Don't worry – there will ALWAYS be someone who isn't going to be happy with what you have sold them. The more people you sell to, the higher the number of dissatisfied customers, even though the percentage stays the same. But here's the easy solution: you only need to offer some form of recompense whenever you make a promise. The most common way to do this is a MONEY-BACK GUARANTEE. Include 'no questions asked' when you give it, and you'll make it even stronger. Other forms of recompense could be a replacement, a repair, or a repeat of a service. Don't waste time or risk bad publicity by disputing any complaint, even if you are certain that person's being unreasonable. Your promise and your guarantee will have gained you more successes, which will far outweigh the losses. Hey, if that isn't the case, you'll need to think about redesigning your product or service. And providing resolution to any dissatisfied customer will make them even more likely to recommend you to others.

Make sure you don't *over-promise* – you have to be sure you are able to deliver what you are promising. And make any caveats clear – in your terms and conditions, or in your communication with the client – if other factors beyond your control need to be taken into consideration. For example, when we are pitching to work at a trade show, we might guarantee a set number of badge swipes and a number of new appointments booked on that day, but we'll make it clear that if there are less than X number of visitors to the show that day, the client of course can't call us in on our guarantee.

EXTRA IMPACT

Alongside all your marketing and selling, aim to make enough impact in your market to keep other people telling everyone else about what you do. It's about taking so much action and making so much noise about what you do that all the right people know about it. On social media, in blogs, on your website, at trade events, meetings and social events – everywhere. BE SEEN AND BE HEARD. This is the reason we got our monster opportunity in Dubai – enough people know who we are and what we do. Even if they've never seen us perform, they've heard about it from other people. It takes time to get to that point, but if you keep taking enough action and creating enough noise, you will get there.

It's also about delivering with authority. Watching Trevor Liley in a meeting is a thing of beauty. He just keeps adding value every step of the way, while everyone is scribbling down everything he is promising to deliver, and he doesn't even mention the price till the end of the meeting. At the end they say, 'WE WANT ALL THAT – WHAT'S THE PRICE?' Trevor just keeps talking about the bigger picture – what he's going to do, what it's going to achieve for them, how much they're going to get out of it, what their returns are going to be, what other people are going to say about them – everything he's talking about is positive, irresistible value to the client, about everything that they're going to gain. If they hesitate, saying they have already overspent their budget, Trevor will say, 'I'm sure you have. But are you spending that money, or are you investing it? We're going to *teach* you how to invest it'. Note there that he doesn't say 'We're going to tell you' . . . 'We're going to *teach* you'. He's coming from such a confident place, with such authority, that he's going to teach them how to invest their money. And they make that investment.

Build extra impact into everything else in your WIDIFY, and it's going to be very difficult for anyone to say no to what you are offering.

FORGET THE SALES PITCH – DELIVER AN EXPERIENCE

One of the best bits of business advice we can give to anybody is to always create an experience, no matter what they are selling. When someone meets you, they may not remember your product, but they will always remember how you made them feel. When they leave, you want them to tell other people about you. That will happen because you were personable, you were different, and you were genuinely enthusiastic about your product. If you talk about your product or your service with enough passion, they will be able to connect with it. Then who are they going to do business with? You. Because you understood them and created a positive experience.

Something we experienced recently really stuck in our minds. We went to a bar where a barman was creating some crazy kind of candy floss on top of our drinks. It was a totally new experience, and now we're talking about it. We took photos and posted them on social media. Even though it took him longer to make that drink, we bought into it, and we went away and told other people about it. We've even put it in this book. If we'd been ten-deep at the bar and only trying to order a beer, we'd have been thinking about getting closer to the bar to see what he was doing. Then, by the time we got to the front, we'd have been wanting everyone else to see what he was doing for us. That barman might be on minimum wage, but he can now increase his income by going for a different job, in a better bar, and saying 'Here's what I do – I sell an experience', instead of being just another barman who can serve drinks.

You need to go to your client and sell your product or your brand with a much more impactful and emotionally charged experience than the three guys who preceded you. You've got to connect with your product enough to be able to say, 'YOU KNOW WHAT, WHAT WE'VE GOT IS DIFFERENT BECAUSE . . . '. You believe in it because you use it, or because you've seen it used, or you've got amazing testimonials or referrals. You've got a story to tell about other people who have benefited from it, in your marketplace.

We sell to a wedding client based purely on emotions, on connectivity and about how they feel. We won't necessarily talk about money until such time that we're thinking, 'If they don't buy into me after that, they probably never will. I've shown them everything I've got to give. If they don't want me now, their decision is based purely on finance, and they can't afford me.'

You've got to sell without being salesy – everyone's had the hard sell from someone else, and it can be the biggest turn-off. You've got to make what you do fun, interesting and more engaging than it will ordinarily be, so that people are more likely to respond to you, then you'll be the one that stands out above the others. While we were researching for this book, Andy Larmouth told us about a locksmith he knows, who carries around a standard lock barrel. He shows people how quickly and easily he can pick the lock, which makes a POWERFUL EMOTIONAL CONNECTION – the fear when people realise how easily someone could break into their house. It's a simple but compelling, visual experience they'll remember and keep thinking about later. Even if they don't sign up there and then, it's almost inevitable that he'll be the first locksmith they think of when they need to get their locks changed.

We are both 100% confident that implementing the advice in this chapter will enable you to make significant improvements to how you feel about selling your product and to your sales conversion rates. THAT'S A PROMISE. Losing your fear and feeling at ease with selling will give you the confidence to deliver an experience with passion and impact. Above all, please spend time perfecting your WIFM, WIDIFY and PET approaches, as well as identifying your WhySPs, and you will see remarkable results in no time at all.

Closely linked to selling is how you manage your money, including deciding on pricing and learning how to understand and increase your value. We'll cover all that in the next chapter.

ILSA HAWTIN COPYWRITER AND COPY-EDITOR – on WhySPs

When I first started working for myself, I really struggled with the advice I kept hearing, that every business needed to have at least one unique selling point.

The classic example of this working is the USP from Domino's: 'Fresh hot pizza delivered to your door in 30 minutes or less . . . or it's free'. Pizza consumers in Michigan had been feeling frustrated by their pizza delivery times, and the catchphrase catapulted Domino's from a small franchise business to the world's second-largest pizza chain. Business sources still recommend remodelling that USP to one that's relevant to your company.

But wait a minute – that USP was created in 1973, when the marketplace was surely very different from today? Globalisation and population levels have vastly increased competition, and customers' demands and expectations have changed accordingly. There are thousands of pizza providers with endless different marketing tactics, and consumers expect fresher ingredients, different types and shapes of pizza, health- and allergy-compliance, etc. *And* speedy delivery.

At least pizza delivery companies can focus on local markets. I can work with clients anywhere in the world – how could the thousands of companies offering services similar to mine all have found a unique and outstanding selling point?

I decided to ditch the USP and to focus on *all* the different points that make me and my services attractive to my target market. I worked most of this out in my mind and transferred it to my marketing, but it's only since working with Spencer and Lee that I have really defined everything on mind maps. I put 'WhySPs' in the middle, to keep my focus on why all the points would appeal to my target customers.

MY ATTRIBUTES	MY WhySPs
Extensive copy-editing/ copywriting training and experience	Superior quality of work, with guaranteed satisfaction and ROI
Multilingual (→ deeper understanding of English)	
Professional and perfectionist approach	
Glowing testimonials and referrals 100% passion for my work	
Many years working in a variety of roles, industries and countries, including management and business-development positions	Solid commercial and business skills, improving my understanding of the client's business and customer requirements
Two-year business management training in Germany	
Five years' copywriting experience, with and measurable results	Copywriting ROI and improved business results
Ability to work outside standard work hours	Fulfilment of diverse and urgent work requirements
Willingness to consider just about any new work request and to work with different requirements and parameters	
Years working in customer-focused environments	First-class customer service, including suggestions to improve clients' own businesses
Knowledge and advice relevant to my clients' own customers	

MY ATTRIBUTES	MY WhySPs
Volunteer work in a listening role, with extensive and regular training	Enjoyable research into clients' business development, including their own WIDIFYs and WhySPs
100% dedication and commitment to my work and clients	Reliability and quality
Broad variety of life experiences Honest, positive and forward-thinking mindset Indomitable spirit	Creative and enriching work experience
Early independence in life Challenging work life experience Strong work ethic	Resilience and reliability
Nearly two years working with Lee Smith and Spencer Wood	Revolutionary approach to business development and success

So, ten strong WhySPs. I'm not going to hand out laminated copies of this table or try and tell everyone about everything I'm offering. I'm not trying to claim that any of those WhySPs are unique, but I strongly doubt that there is a copy-editor or copywriter who can offer all those selling points. Especially the final one.

Above all, seeing all my selling points written down and knowing how legitimate they all are gives me a whole new level of confidence in what I am offering and how I can help my clients. And as soon as I find out what is most important to a specific client, e.g. reliability or quality or ROI, I can tell them about my respective WhySPs – why they want to employ my copy-editing and/or copywriting services.

CHAPTER 7

Money, money, money

A surprising number of the people we meet feel anxious about managing the money side of their business. They focus hard on perfecting their product, developing their service, creating publicity and delivering well to their customers. But they seem to do anything to avoid talking about money, instead blindly hoping they'll generate enough income to pay the bills and that their accountant will sort everything else out.

THERE'S NO WAY AROUND THIS: YOU HAVE GOT TO KNOW YOUR NUMBERS.

Anyone who has ever watched *Dragons' Den* knows how true that statement is. You need to be sure about – and keep re-evaluating – what you want and where you need to be regarding the prices you charge and the goals you set yourself. This chapter will give you practical tips on a positive approach towards managing your money flow, from understanding and increasing your value, to how and why you need to set goals.

You'll see a strong emphasis on how you can increase your income. As we stated in Chapter 2, you have to define success on your own terms, but we hope we can safely assume you wouldn't be reading this book if you didn't in some way want to improve your business in order to earn more money. We obviously can't tell you here what you should be charging for your product or what goals you need to set for yourself. But we will tell you how you can make improvements on your own terms, in order to increase your income and to feel in control of your finances.

UNDERSTAND YOUR VALUE AND SET YOUR PRICES

Both of us believe strongly that the majority of owners of small or medium-sized businesses undervalue themselves, their products and their services. Most people we've worked with have admitted to worrying about what they should be charging and how much their customers will be able to afford or be willing to pay. Here's the first important point in this chapter: when deciding on pricing, DON'T TRY

TO SECOND-GUESS ANYONE'S BUDGET. You need to understand and set your own value and your own market, based on the value of what you deliver and what you want to achieve. A budget is usually only a reflection of the amount of money that has previously been spent on a particular product or service, and put in place to give purchasers some parameters. Even if someone tells you they have a strict budget, there is nearly always room for manoeuvre. If you WIDIFY the process, add value, deliver a solution with impact and offer a guarantee, it's very likely that a client will be more than willing to invest more than they originally anticipated.

When Spencer first started performing magic, while it was still a working hobby for him, most magicians he knew would take on just about any job for what was effectively only beer vouchers. They'd be enjoying a night out at a nice venue, with a few drinks thrown in, getting paid next to nothing to do a few tricks. It soon became clear to Spencer that those magicians were devaluing the product, themselves and what they did. Not only that, but they were determining their future client base . . . and the client bases of other magicians.

Spencer took an entirely different approach. He valued his own time – hey, if he was going to go out and leave his partner on a Saturday night, even if only a couple of times a month at this stage, he would only do it for the money that he felt justified his time. He knew that he was going to be entertaining a venue's clients, thereby increasing the return to the venue's business and income. He valued his skillset and was confident that he was good enough to charge the right price, irrespective of what anyone else's impression of him might be.

The most important point to note here is that Spencer didn't end up with more Saturday nights in. Quite the opposite – he very soon gained a reputation as a successful magician, and the demand for his performances escalated. Soon the strength of his client base was apparent – venues that had the money to spend and knew the positive impact Spencer was having on their own business was worth the price he was charging. Not only that, but the positive effect of earning good money for every gig improved Spencer's own performance – we all know how much better we feel and perform when we are being paid more by a high-end client. A *MAGIC VORTEX.*

Lee's approach when he first started performing magic was slightly different, but with the same end result. Thanks to his non-stop networking, he soon started to pass on work to other magicians, retaining the higher-end jobs for himself. He noticed the same surprising effect as soon as he started to increase his prices – he couldn't believe how much faster the enquiries were coming in and how many were converting. He was having to do considerably less work for more money and started being able to pick and choose, as he got double-booked or even triple-booked for the following year. Lee agrees that PRICING IS ALL ABOUT CONFIDENCE. When he's busy, he doesn't need to worry about what's coming in next year, giving him more confidence to stand firm on the price at which he values himself.

Spencer says, 'You can always negotiate down from the price on the table. It's a damned sight harder to negotiate up, so you might as well start off asking for more – you've got nothing to lose. Just ask for the price you want to receive; if they decline, at least there is an amount payable on the table to allow for the "wiggle". LET THE NEGOTIATIONS BEGIN.'

We have already learnt a lot from each other on this, about the power of non-stop networking, and the importance of increasing the value of what we do. Both of us keep getting enquiries for work two or three years ahead . . . which leads us to another sticking point that we need to help you overcome. We simply cannot understand it when a business owner declines an order or booking more than a few months away, simply because they don't yet know what their prices will be. Are they mad?

We'll tell you all about setting goals later in this chapter, but in short for now: all you need to do is think how much you want to grow and quote for how much you will be charging in the future. If you're charging £XYZ now and you know that in two years you are aiming to have grown your business by 30%, quote now for £XYZ + 30% FOR ANY BOOKING IN TWO YEARS. You don't know if you will actually have grown 30% by then, but unless you make a positive decision now, you'll be ensuring you don't.

MAKE A DECISION AND GO WITH IT.

Even if the customer then doesn't buy at that price, you won't be worse off than if you hadn't made them an offer. And the chances are very high that, by not undervaluing yourself, you will increase the likelihood of them returning to invest with you at a later date. You may well have experienced this in reverse, when a client has chosen someone else over you, even though your prices were lower – it's happened to both of us a number of times. Again, it just goes to show that money isn't always (or even often) the deciding factor. Don't worry about losing the job on price – money will rarely be the deciding factor. Worry about losing only because your WIDIFY didn't work, because you didn't offer enough value, or you didn't deliver an impactful experience. The best example we have of this is when Spencer lost a massive opportunity to another performer because his WIDIFY wasn't in place. The other performer, Nick Crown, not only offered less in time and overall content, but he then charged more for the pleasure. GO FIGURE.

We are both fans of earning good money, and Spencer especially isn't a fan of doing something for nothing without good reason, feeling strongly that it doesn't breed credibility in him as an individual. Spencer simply never doubts his skillset and his own ability. These days, he is less likely to do anything for free when he first steps out of his comfort zone – he says he might as well charge *more* than normal, increasing credibility in himself right away, rather than not charging just because he's never done it before. In the past, when he did a charity gig for free, he swears he could feel a different level of respect in the room and from the organiser. While he was at the event, he felt he'd lost his 'READY BREK GLOW' – because he was there for free, he wasn't performing with his normal (abnormal) levels of energy and charisma.

If a client is surprised by a price that Spencer quotes, he tells them, 'Well, it's taken 15 years for me to get to the point where I can charge that much. You can of course book the guy who's only been doing it for 12 months, who's going to charge you a third of my price. If he does a good job, that's a result. If he does a bad job, you'll wish you had invested the extra money to book me.' This type of response is all that much easier when you know your numbers, which gives you increased confidence in selling yourself better, despite the risk of you not getting the job. But we're back to the *MAGIC VORTEX* . . . the more you increase your prices, if only gradually at first, the more your confidence will grow and the more you will be able to charge.

Changing your prices will almost certainly require (or lead to) changes to your client base. You might be able to gradually increase your price, but existing customers will be unwilling or unable to pay substantially more than you have been charging them to date, even if you increase the value of what you are delivering.

For any product or service in the world, there will always be a clear-cut range of client bases. If you are now charging £500, there will be clients you may have already outgrown, who would only pay up to £300 for what you do. There will be a crowd who can afford £300–£500, and there will be a group that pays just about any amount higher than that. That last group is smaller in size, but as long as you want to keep growing your business and increasing your income, you need to keep looking for ways in which you can ultimately start selling to those high-end clients. It's worth noting that these are people who aren't happy to pay less – they want to be able to tell their friends about the impressive investment they have made. Spencer tells a story of a plastic surgeon he met, who was so busy and in such demand from his particular client base, that he had his own helicopter to fly him around the country to meet with the ever-growing list of referrals. Our clients love to share with others how far they have reached out to find us and that they have paid us more than any local entertainer. It breeds credibility in the client's decision-making process to use only the best, and that their guests or clients only deserve to be entertained by the best.

LIFE GOAL: GET YOURSELF A HELICOPTER AND SOMEONE ELSE TO FLY YOU AROUND IN IT.

It's also worth noting that the high-end market is the hardest to penetrate. You might not even know who those clients are or how you can contact them – you will probably have to keep working on improving your brand and image until they come and find you. But isn't that an exciting challenge, as something to keep working towards? For now, you need to remember that it's not until you start separating the serious bookings from the budget-conscious, whilst increasing your prices, that you will be able to move into that market. Once you start getting bigger jobs and higher-end clients . . . it's back to the *MAGIC VORTEX*.

For anyone who is thinking this sounds ruthless, please stop and think again. **No one is forcing anyone to pay any price.** There will always be hundreds of other people or businesses offering a similar product or service for less money, which the client can choose if they can't or don't want to afford you. You don't have to strive to charge more than you are worth, and you don't have to ditch customers you personally value just because you have decided to increase your charges beyond their budget. But you do need to keep positively re-evaluating yourself, your product and your service, in order to keep increasing your income and your business. Undervaluing yourself immediately reduces the credibility of you and your business.

ADD VALUE

When you are providing a proposal, don't forget all the points from the last chapter – even if someone at first thinks that you are outside their budget, you need to show them why you do it for them (your WIDIFY), to put so much value on what you do that the vision of buying from you outweighs the financial cost. If the value exceeds the price, they will invest every time.

We also need to shed a different light on the first important point we raised in this chapter, that you shouldn't be trying to second-guess how much money other people have. THE KEY WORD THERE IS 'GUESS'.

When you *know* that a client has a bigger budget, or the ability to stretch their budget, you can of course charge more. Again, this isn't about being ruthless – you're not going to be charging more for exactly the same product. If you have an enquiry from a high-end client, look at every way possible that you can add value to what you would otherwise offer, in order to be able to charge more. You might be able to upsell another product or an extra service. You could double the time you'll spend at their event, or improve the delivery experience for your product. Whatever your line of business, there will be numerous ways you can increase the value of your product or service in order to boost your revenue when dealing with clients who have a larger potential budget.

If you are selling a service, it's important to remember that YOU DON'T HAVE TO HAVE A SET RATE, for example the amount you charge per hour or per day. We can both charge as much for an hour's training as for a day at a trade show, for instance, by making sure that the client's sales team is fully prepared for the day ahead. The value to the client, having his team fully revved up and able to sell ten times better than usual, could even outweigh the value of having one of us at the event all day.

THINK BIGGER

We needed to get you used to the idea of how and why you can increase your prices before taking you back to the ideal foundation to enable it to happen: the mindset of thinking bigger. The order of this chapter is how it happened for both of us, but we're going to give you the advantage of knowing from the start how your mindset will make a massive difference.

Now that we are both enjoying solid levels of income and working with higher-end clients, we realise that it was only when we really started to think bigger and set higher goals that everything started to change dramatically for us. As soon as we set ourselves higher goals, we implemented the measures and processes required to reach them. We would even challenge each other to gain a certain client or contract, which is another benefit of the Buddy Up System we will tell you more about in Chapter 11. Then we kept thinking bigger, each time simply setting higher goals, then working out what we had to do to get there.

We now set ourselves the challenge of achieving a 'MONSTER' every single year – the job where we can earn more in a day than we would even have thought possible only a few years ago. Our biggest Monster to date was to perform for 90 seconds at the opening night of the DAMAC Hills and Trump International Golf Club in Dubai. We didn't go out worrying about justifying the price we charged – we had decided what we wanted to charge for the job and that we were worth it. Sometimes you absolutely have to be ready to push the boundaries and take a risk.

Another example of a risk paying off was when we were working for an international cosmetics brand. We had already upped the game, increasing the initial two days' work to a three-month contract, culminating in a global product launch. Three months of performing to employees, the press, bloggers, vloggers and VIP guests, on a specially commissioned boat on the Thames in London. On the final morning, the global CEO flew in from San Francisco . . . and Spencer suddenly decided to raise the bar by making a last-minute change to the performance we had been delivering every day for three months. Just a few minutes before we arrived, we grabbed a dictionary from Waterstones, to make the final trick all around arriving at the name of the company in this huge dictionary. It was a high-risk strategy, and the client looked white as we started the trick differently from how she was expecting. But we nailed it. The response was unreal – the room full of over 100 people erupted, the CEO thought we were awesome and our client hasn't stopped recommending us ever since to other high-end clients and brands.

From now on, work towards setting yourself new, higher goals at every stage of your business development. Aim to sell more, increase a client's investment, secure a new client – whatever will make your business more successful. Make sure you find out what you need to do to reach each goal, for example finding out what will help you to sell a higher package with more added value. And don't be afraid of taking risks – they won't always work, but when they do, the results will be phenomenal. The most important point to remember at all times: THINKING BIGGER AUTOMATICALLY MAKES YOU SET YOUR GOALS HIGHER AND ALLOWS YOU TO ACHIEVE MORE.

KNOW YOUR STUFF

You are simply never going to reach your full potential – your highest possible business income – unless you have a few things very clear in your mind. What are your numbers, i.e. your net income, cash flow, turnover, profit levels and expenses? What are your long-term targets and your goals? What is your soft target for the year, which you'll have to work hard to achieve? What is your hard target, where falling just short of it will still be a big success? This might feel like a scary list of questions, but they are all questions that you need to have the answers for. It might take you some time to work it all out, but after that it will take little effort for you to keep on top of your numbers as your business and your goals change.

Spencer benefited fairly early on from advice from a business mentor, who asked everything about his income, including his targets, then explained how Spencer simply wouldn't ever be able to reach his target income without increasing his prices. With the gig average he had at that time, he would have needed to do over 250 gigs in a year, which is virtually impossible with all of life's usual factors in play, including the time needed to generate new business. His mentor immediately made it clear, just by looking at the numbers, that Spencer needed to increase his prices, i.e. his gig average, in order to achieve a higher income.

It is just as important for any business owner to work on an average monthly income, based on the entire year. We both know too many performers who enjoy a great income each year in December, one of the peak months for performers. They then splash out on something they've been wanting for a while, while not worrying too much about the quieter months immediately after Christmas. Then suddenly they find themselves worrying in Q1 because they haven't got enough money coming in.

You need to average out your whole annual income over 12 months, in order to know for sure that you are earning enough over the whole year. Learn to pay yourself like a business – a set amount – instead of living on what you earn each month. This will immediately give you more stability and security, with no highs or lows in your business, because you will have an equal balance across an entire period of time. Plan to earn enough to stay in advance of all your expenses, instead of getting behind them. Aim to get one year ahead of your bills and your payments. INCREASE YOUR ZERO BALANCE, i.e. the minimum you want to retain in your bank account. Then, after you've paid all your bills every month, ending with a higher zero balance, set yourself a new goal for a *higher* zero balance for the next month. You can even get to the point where you stop thinking about what your business is worth over a year, and start to think of it as your career. Then you won't get to the end of December and think that you're starting from zero again. Your business doesn't stop at the end of 12 months – it's just keeps rolling on for the number of years until you are able to retire. Ultimately, your mindset will even change to 'no days off' – the week never starts and never ends, and the year is everlasting.

Every business is different, but you get the idea – you've got to know your numbers, and you've got to know how much you earn per month and per year. You need to know what your unit price or monthly average is and drive that figure upwards. You need to keep on top of your numbers and keep setting goals, in order to avoid stress and to keep increasing your levels of success. IF YOU DON'T KNOW YOUR NUMBERS, YOU WILL NOT BE ABLE TO GROW YOUR BUSINESS.

SET GOALS

We've touched on the importance of setting goals throughout this book and in this chapter. It's not rocket science, but we now want to share some of the tricks that have helped us to maximise our own goals.

We'll start by telling you how to work out YOUR MAGIC NUMBER, which will come somewhere in between your soft and hard targets – a goal you can definitely achieve if you take enough action. It could be very close to your full-time income in a PAYE job, you could base it on the income you have earned from your previous year in business, or you could take the last six months of your business income and double that figure. Now let's stretch that figure by 40%, to make it a bit more exciting. Then add another 10% – extra income for you to be able to enjoy a few of life's luxuries. That gives you your magic number, your hard target. Your soft target, i.e. the minimum you must aim to achieve, could be your previous year's income, plus an extra 10% or 20%. It's as simple as that.

We consider it essential to have both a soft and a hard target. If you pitch up anywhere in between the two, you can be satisfied you've had a good year. If you don't set those targets, you probably won't even reach the soft target that you would have set yourself. Striving each year to reach a target will automatically make you do things you wouldn't otherwise do. You'll have to steer everything in your business around aiming for the target. Your levels of drive will change, from just getting by, to striving to reach your new goal. You'll start adapting new business approaches that you otherwise wouldn't have seriously considered. You'll meet other, more successful people, who give you the motivation and/or channels to increase your income. THINGS WILL JUST HAPPEN, AS LONG AS YOU ARE TRYING TO HIT THAT TARGET. We could set a target to perform for monkeys living on the moon. It's never going to happen, but we are happy that aiming for the target might just land us a job with NASA.

Once you have set your soft and hard targets, you need to work out what you need to do to get there – how much more business, how many new clients, how big an increase in your prices. It's very likely you're going to need to venture out of your comfort zone, into a new area you've been thinking about (or trying not to think about) for some time. Whatever it is, you mustn't sit there and think about how hard it's going to be – you simply need to decide that you are going to do whatever you need to do in order to reach your target. If you start off doubting your ability, it won't happen. As long as you stay determined and positive, you'll experience the *MAGIC VORTEX* effect – your increased activity levels will increase your workload, and vice versa.

Just as vital as setting your income targets and your monthly zero balance, is setting a target for the money you want to have in the bank before you start the following year. At the time of writing, we both set that target as our living expenses plus 30% for next year – even if we packed up shop, we would be able survive very happily for at least one year before requiring additional income. If you're feeling successful because you've got a few thousand pounds in the bank going into the following year, we encourage you to re-evaluate and aim higher.

If you have hit your soft target and are satisfied with what you have in the bank before you start the next year, you might be tempted to lower your monthly average, by accepting lower prices or offering discounts. **Think again.** When you are in a truly secure financial position, you can benefit from the confidence that brings, and try for higher prices. Turn down the lower-priced opportunities, knowing it's more likely than ever you will be able to secure other, higher-priced contracts. This also gives you the foundation for your Monster. If you go into your financial year without much new business lined up, you'll sell your soul when it comes to any big job. But if you go into that year with all your living costs plus 30% banked, the dynamic of how you sell will change. You can hold your price, and you will already feel more confidence in increasing what you charge.

Even when you haven't yet hit your soft target, we encourage you to AVOID OFFERING DISCOUNTS. If you're offering a service for £500 and someone says they've only got £450, say to them, 'Great – all you need to do is find an extra £50. How exciting is that, to know that you are only £50 from being able to book me? It's exciting times. I'm excited for you. All you've got to do is get off this phone and rally round with a few of your pals, get £50 together in coppers and coins, pounds and pence, and you'll be able to book me. And I'm going to smash it – your event is going to rock. That's a great solution to have.' Those are Spencer's words, which you can adapt for your own business. This whole pitch is a lot of fun to deliver and usually gets a chuckle from the other person as soon as they twig what you have just done. It works especially well when the gap between their price and yours isn't too big; the tactics change as the gap between the two figures increases.

If a potential customer asks if there is any movement on the price, reply 'YES, UPWARDS'. Don't say what nine out of ten business people would: 'Well, what are you thinking?'. The next thing you know, you'll be accepting half your original price. The client will be wondering if they should have asked for more off, and they will have already lost some respect for you or your product. It might sound brutal, but you've just got to learn to say 'no'. Please trust us on this – in the long run you will only regret offering discounts. IF YOU'RE GENUINELY HAPPY TO OFFER ONE, TAKE THAT MONEY OFF BEFORE YOU GO IN.

We both have less fear now of losing a job. If we do, we know it's because it's the one time out of ten where the client didn't have the money. We would rather lose a job because someone can't afford us than if they've preferred someone else or someone else has sold it better. We've both received emails from clients who say we were three times as expensive as someone else, but no one competed with what we were offering. They parted with the extra money because of the extra *value* we put on what we deliver.

Goals don't have to be purely financial. Whether money is a main driving factor for you or not, you will at some point have something else you want to achieve, for any number of reasons. It might be a personal conquest, say wanting to achieve something you only used to dream about achieving. It could be a goal with a different outcome, for purely personal fulfilment, for example helping a certain number of people by providing them with employment or training. It could be for a charitable cause, or because you want to be able to move into a new area of work you think you will enjoy more. Whatever your motives, don't ever doubt your ability to achieve your goals. Make them clear and strong in your mind and decide that you ARE going to achieve them, no matter what happens.

YOU CAN'T JUST DECIDE ON A GOAL AND SIT BACK AND WAIT FOR IT TO HAPPEN, and you mustn't get comfortable with where you are. You need to go out there and find more all the time; if you get complacent, you will soon have a month of less activity. At the time of writing, Spencer's main ambition is to develop his speaking career. He has read books and written pages and pages of notes linked to his goal of being a speaker, from titles of talks to introductions and quotes, to the tricks he'll do when he's on stage. He's investigated all the other aspects of business that could be beneficial from an audience-interactive perspective. He knows he's going to be a successful speaker, and he's putting all the stepping stones in place to enable himself to get there.

Whatever you want to achieve, simply start putting things in place to get there. Even if you initially only get out of bed one hour earlier, so that you can start finding out more about what you need to do to achieve your goal. Work out your financial targets and firmly resolve to achieve the soft target you have set yourself. Set out the smaller goals you need to achieve on a daily, weekly, monthly or yearly plan so you can continue to move towards your end goal. Then keep writing your end goal down, keep thinking about it, keep driving it, and it's almost inevitable that you will one day get there.

SPEND YOUR MONEY!

There's almost nothing more annoying than buying a round of drinks when you're out with someone who you know is never going to reach for their wallet. You must know people like that, and there will be at least one person reading this who never offers to buy a round. If it's you, you know who you are. Stop it, now. That might have sounded like a personal gripe. Don't worry, we're not going to name and shame anyone, we just might not want to go for a drink with you. And seriously, there is a very important reason for us raising the point in this book.

It really is hard to enjoy doing business with anyone who hates parting with their cash. Apart from it being annoying if you're the one who always picks up the coffee tab, you naturally assume the other person wouldn't be generous enough to share business with you. If someone isn't willing to invest in their website or marketing, they lack credibility as a successful businessperson. When you know someone focuses on avoiding any small costs, you can't help but assume they're not earning much money from their business. It's normal to ask if there's room for movement on an expensive deal, but your respect for another businessperson drains when they keep wanting to haggle over £50 – money that isn't going to have any significant impact on the success of their company.

YOU NEED TO BE WILLING TO INVEST IN ORDER TO GROW, and we're not talking only about the money you invest directly into your business. For example, we both sometimes meet with clients that we know are multimillionaires. They may be earning considerably more than us but, if we've called the meeting or we stand to gain more from it than they will, there's no way we will ever let them pay for lunch. Over the years, we've both taken work from other magicians, and we have never raised an objection to giving them commission for the work they've given us. Hey, if you don't show any appreciation for the work someone's giving you, it's less likely they'll contact you next time they have a work overload.

While we are both keen to increase our income, neither of us worries about small everyday expenses – we're sure that would only cost us more in the long run. Everyone has worries about money at different increments, and there are times in every business lifecycle when you have to budget more carefully. Just don't be the person who always finds an excuse to avoid unnecessary expenses.

THIS MIGHT BE SOUNDING NEGATIVE – LET'S TURN IT AROUND. We all know the relaxed, generous people in life who have a positive outlook. They don't quibble over small invoices, they pay on time and they generally bring a stress-free experience to the table. They come across as successful in what they are doing, they appreciate you and they're a pleasure to do business with. Lose the short-arms-deep-pockets syndrome, join the generous group, and you will experience the positive effects.

This has been the longest chapter yet, so here's a short, sharp summary of all the points we've raised. Master these, and you'll soon be in control of the money side of your business.

1. Stop underestimating yourself and what you have to offer
2. Set your prices accordingly, and always be ready to re-evaluate and charge more
3. Keep looking for ways to add value to your product or service and increase your prices
4. Get used to thinking bigger, then you will automatically achieve more
5. Get to grips with all your numbers
6. Set yourself goals and targets, in just about everything you do
7. Don't be a tightwad

We're going to finish this chapter with an interview from a good friend of ours, the brilliant performer and all-round good guy, Andy Larmouth. Andy did something we never had the guts to do, taking the plunge to become a full-time magician before feeling certain that he could make a substantial income from magic in order to support his family. He was also a bloody good sport when we ripped him to shreds over a price he'd quoted for a gig in his hometown of Middlesbrough. If you are after an excellent magician – and if we're already booked – we highly recommend you call Andy. Just don't expect him to give you a discount. The following transcript is from a recent follow-up conversation with him.

INTERVIEW WITH ANDY LARMOUTH – MAGICIAN

What gave you the nerve to take the plunge?

I don't know, really – it was more reckless than brave. I used to teach the guitar and I really enjoyed it at first, but the education system has changed so much – it got to the point where teaching felt more like babysitting. I became deeply unhappy with the situation I was in and just couldn't see a way out. At the time, I was performing magic in my spare time and I'd started to get a few more magic gigs in – restaurants and the odd wedding. Then one day, I just decided to go for it. I expected my parents to think I was making a big mistake. They've always been supportive, but my dad can still be my biggest critic. They seem really impressed by what I'm doing now, and it's made a massive difference, having their support. I can't believe it sometimes, that I'm now making a really good income from full-time magic.

I still teach guitar for one day a week. It started off as a safety net, in case magic didn't work out for me, but that has changed. Not only do I keep my hand in with playing guitar, but it keeps me grounded, appreciating where I am now. The difference in atmosphere is phenomenal – my whole headspace, knowing that during that time I am answerable to someone else. Then from 3.15 that day for the whole of the rest of the week, I can do exactly what I want. It is such a liberating and empowering feeling. I wonder if people who have always worked for someone else can realise how that feels.

How did you find it when you first went full-time into magic?

There just wasn't a market where I live, at least not in quality magicians at the events I perform at now, and it was really hard at first, starting from scratch. But focusing on creating relationships made the biggest difference then. I just kept arranging meetings, networking, going to wedding fairs – anything and anyone I could think of. I have a simple formula: don't be a wally [he used a stronger word than that]. If you are nice and genuine with people, it pays off. I make my money from performing magic, but the magic isn't the main thing – it's about being a positive presence at an event, getting on with people and making that event better for the people I'm working with. Now I'm getting more and more enquiries, from referrals and recommendations, and I'm taking bookings for three years from now.

Have you changed your pricing since our meeting?!

Definitely. You're going to kill me again now, but I still did that booking, the one for the low price that you're never going to let me forget. I don't regret doing the gig, and I still get good feedback on Facebook from that group. But since that time, it's like I can hear you two in my head every time I'm taking a booking.

Money has never really been the main driving factor for me, I have to admit. But I've got a family to support, and I know I've got to think more long-term about finances. And there's such a buzz from being able to buy things you couldn't have afforded just a year ago. Say, I've got this new campervan, and the satisfaction of seeing it there on my drive and knowing that I paid for it by doing magic tricks – it's ridiculous!

Talking to you about all this honestly made the biggest difference ever to my business. It's not that I didn't value myself before that; it's about having the confidence, really KNOWING what I'm worth. It's just something that doesn't come naturally to most people – they should teach it in school. As soon as you decide what you are worth, you have so much more confidence. I used to feel uncomfortable stating my price, and found myself offering discounts before people had even asked for one! Now I tell anyone what I charge with absolute confidence – I don't expect them to question it. If they do, I have all the ways to back it up, telling them about the value I'm going to add and the difference I'll make to their event.

Not long after our meeting, someone asked if I would give a discount for cash for a wedding three years from now. As I was talking, I could hear the difference in what I was saying: 'No, I can't give you a discount. Not only that, your wedding is three years from now, so you're actually getting a massive bargain right now – who knows what my prices will be by then.' Not only did that couple still book me, they changed from two hours to booking me for their entire day. Unbelievable. I was speaking with more confidence, that's the major difference.

After our meeting, I set myself a new financial goal for the year, April to April. It's now October, and I've already exceeded that goal in the bookings I've taken. I'm really happy with where I am now, but I know now that I need to feel satisfied without being complacent – I need to keep setting myself higher goals.

CHAPTER 8

Get on top, stay on top

There will always be new things you can (and need to) do to keep improving and increasing your business. JUST BEING BUSY IS LIKE RUNNING ON A TREADMILL – it doesn't matter how fast your legs are moving, you're still going nowhere. In all the meetings we had while researching for this book, we identified the techniques that have contributed the most to our success in business, most of which grouped together smartly to form ten chapters. This is the bonus chapter – 15 extra nuggets, each as powerful as any section in the other chapters. You'll see a strong emphasis on efficiency – smart ways to cut time while staying on top of the processes that will keep your business running smoothly. Above all, we will also encourage you to keep thinking outside the box, to think creatively in order to find innovative solutions. This is something magicians are renowned for – it's crucial to our profession – but unconventional thinking is something that anyone can learn and develop.

The 15 points make up a lot of information to take on board, so we have arranged them in the order we think will be most beneficial to you as you develop your business. Please keep referring to all these points – even if they don't feel relevant to you now, you might be very surprised by the positive outcomes when you try implementing them at a later date or stage in your business. We'll round up this chapter with enlightening business advice from the brilliant Dr Shotter, founder of the Illuminate Skin Clinics, and a naturally talented entrepreneur.

BUCKLE UP.

PLANNING YOUR DAY

You no doubt work with one or more calendars, to-do lists and/or apps to help you keep on top of everything, but if you don't already plan every day, we highly recommend you start doing it *today*. It's an easy and enjoyable exercise, and you will be amazed by the increase in your motivation and productivity.

Here are the key points to planning your day:

- **Always plan one day ahead.** If you wake up thinking about having to take time out to write up your plan, it's likely to feel slightly stressful and/or time-consuming – more like firefighting than planning. We both write up plans in the evening for the next day, when it's clear in our minds what we want and need to achieve. There's nothing tedious about this – it's relaxing time out, making a positive plan.

- **Plan everything to specific times.** This isn't just a to-do list. Whether you're using a blank piece of A4 or Grant Cardone's challenging 10X Planner, make sure that you allot specific times for each action.

- **Plan your whole day.** Decide when you're going to get up, what time you'll have breakfast or go for a run. Allot specific times for answering emails, telemarketing, prospecting, studying, reading, researching new clients – all the things you are going to do that are related to your business. Add breaks during the day, including time for meditation or going to the gym, and slots for any specific chores you need to do. Plan for switch-off time, for example collecting your kids from school and helping with homework, or time to make dinner and catch up with your partner – positive time when you can 100% switch off from work. We highly recommend including time every day for reflection, to write down everything you have achieved that day, as well as a time slot to write your plan for the next day.

You will find yourself naturally prioritising – some people like to get all the small jobs done in the first hour, while others prefer to accomplish a challenging task before taking their first break. It's not catastrophic if you overrun a time slot, especially if you are making good progress in an important task – just add notes to your plan about anything you are postponing. After you've been doing this for a couple of weeks, you'll find yourself planning times more accurately.

Instead of referring to your family's calendar, your own calendar, your notes, to-do lists and emails, etc, we can just about guarantee that having everything in one place will significantly improve your mindset and stress levels. The personal accountability is motivational – instead of lying in bed trying to remember the things you ought to be doing that day, you'll get up feeling positive and empowered to work through your list. While some people will always prefer to do everything electronically, we recommend at least trying this on paper – there is something incredibly satisfying about crossing things off a list; even CEOs of tech firms still keep paper notes for their plans.

PLANNING YOUR BUSINESS

John P Morgan, a life coach and a great friend of Lee's, gives great advice about 'SETTING UP A BUSINESS BACKWARDS'. He talks about knowing people who go out, create their business plans, get all their marketing content sorted and feel that they are then in business. Then they suddenly find themselves with no work and out of pocket, because they focused too early on the front end.

John maintains you need to do everything the other way round – find the thing you're good at, push it to your max, get busy, THEN sort out the rest of your infrastructure. By then, you'll already know whether you have a viable business, and you'll have the income to do all the things you want and need to do to make it even more successful. If you're good at what you do and you keep on doing it the best you can, the work will find you. Don't doubt yourself if anyone questions why you don't yet have a website, for example – tell them confidently that you're not making substantial investments before your business is well established. THEY'LL RESPECT YOU FOR IT.

The one exception here is business cards – they are a very small investment and a great way to make contacts and connections . . .

BUSINESS CARDS

For us, business cards are more important than the playing cards we use to perform magic. We can bet you that, while getting ready for a gig, 90% of other magicians will be focusing hardest on filling their bag with all the gear they need to perform. We will spend more time on our appearance, to create the ideal impression of ourselves and our brands. And we'll only be panicking if we're running short of business cards.

We've met people who say they don't want to give their business cards out because they've only got a few left. WHAT'S THE MENTALITY THERE? Whenever you meet *anyone*, give them your business card. Say 'You might never need me, but I want you to think about me one day', increasing the chances that they will go away and tell someone else about you. The worst that's going to happen is they leave it on the table, in which case someone else might still pick it up. A small investment in a tiny piece of marketing, which can and will one day lead to an important and valuable new connection.

Imagine how beneficial it would be if you got on the train, in the rush hour, and walked up and down the aisle asking for people's business cards. Anyone who's got one can probably afford a high-value contract with you because they're high enough up in their organisation to have a business card . . . and you've now got their contact details. For £30, you could buy a Kindle. Then on the Tube, you tell people you are going to give it away before the next stop, by picking a business card at random from any you collect. Then you've *already* got a connection when you contact any of those people: 'I'm that man on the train who gave a Kindle away. While you didn't win from me this time, you seem like the type of person who would love what my business provides.' You could give away a Kindle an hour and you'd still be quids in if it leads to one significant client.

These are random examples – you might not be the type of person who would feel comfortable approaching a load of commuters on a train, but you get the picture. KEEP THINKING OUTSIDE THE BOX about how you can make new contacts and attract new customers.

Remember to keep focusing in just the same way on making connections with other suppliers, so that they keep selling you to any of their own contacts who are likely to have an interest in what you are providing.

MIND MAPS

Mind mapping is possibly our most powerful tool in developing our businesses, and it's something we do every single day. You probably already have some understanding of how mind mapping works, but it's likely you aren't in the habit of doing it regularly and on every subject, task and project. We hope this section will change that. We can't count the number of people we've met on our journey so far who have been astounded when we've shown them the power of mind mapping.

THE PROCESS IS INCREDIBLY SIMPLE. Take a subject you want to make improvements on and write that subject inside a bubble/circle in the centre of a page. Think of any areas that are related to the central subject, write those words in separate bubbles around the first one, and join each new bubble with a line to the central bubble. Be as creative as you can in this thinking, for example talking it through with friends, asking other magicians, searching on the internet, etc. After that, think of all the areas related to each of the new, outer bubbles and do the same again – new bubbles, each attached to the relevant original bubble.

One of the people we've helped with this process is Max Plathan, a good friend and highly artistic visual designer. She felt that she was getting 'stuck' working on very similar types of commissions and wanted to broaden her line of work, to challenge herself and develop her skills further. Having read an inspiring book by Carol Dweck, *Mindset*, Max had begun to realise there were no limits to what she could achieve, but she was having difficulty identifying which areas would give her the best financial and personal fulfilment.

We worked out the following core mind map together, and Max was surprised by the number of areas of potential new development. She could then easily pinpoint the three most important areas, and you'll see in the second mind map how she expanded on one of those key areas: visual design. She is now focusing her efforts on the key areas of visual design, UX design/research and creative problem solving. Max says that our one-hour mind-mapping exercise made an incredibly positive difference to how she now prioritises work and focuses her efforts.

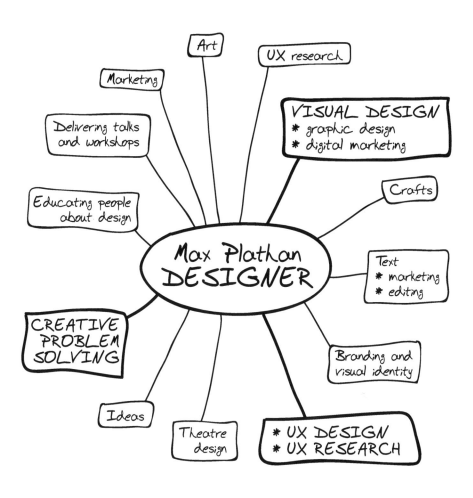

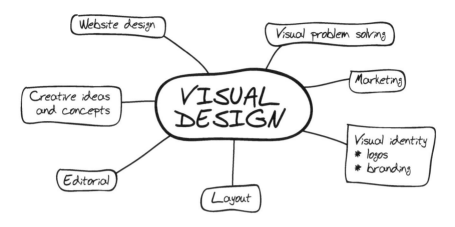

Here are the main five reasons we have gained so much from using mind maps:

1. **Mind maps make your plans visual and real.** When you write down actions you need to take, your brain connects strongly to the reality that you can and will follow up on any points you make. You now have a clear and visual plan of the actions you need to work through to reach your end goal.

2. **Mind mapping makes ideas stick.** If you keep ideas in your head without writing them down, you forget 90% of them, and it's likely you wouldn't take action on the other 10%. Once your thoughts and all the associated ideas and research are on paper, you can keep referring to them and you'll feel motivated to take action. Transfer the data to a mind mapping app and you can keep your new targets with you at all times.

3. **Mind mapping uncovers new opportunities.** Every single time you mind map, you will be more creative, engaging your brain on a deeper level and in completely different ways of considering A) your ideal goals and B) the ways you can achieve them.

4. **The benefits of mind mapping are endless.** Every single time you want to think differently, more creatively and/or more effectively about something, draw up a mind map, think outside the box, take the actions required and start enjoying the results.

5. **You can mind map for *anything*.** Whenever you have any area you want to develop, create a mind map to maximise your success. It's brilliant for setting goals, organising projects, analysing problem areas, exploring a new concept – anything.

WE HOPE YOU'RE NOW STARTING TO REALISE THE ENORMOUS POTENTIAL. We have done mind mapping in every single meeting since we first started working together. We have used it to enter new areas of business and new markets. We built up the content of our most recent seminar project, as well as the ways we would deliver it, using a series of different, ever-evolving mind maps. Following the first STEP System Seminar, we revisited those mind maps and made adjustments, to enable improvements and developments, based on our experiences and the questions and feedback from the participants. WE WON'T FORGET THOSE NEW DEVELOPMENTS – THEY'RE ON A MIND MAP.

This is also the ultimate tool for creating the ultimate sales solution, your WIDIFY. Put mind maps up all over your wall where you work, to enable you to keep thinking creatively, to keep thinking outside the box and reaching new levels. Mind mapping with someone else can double the results. Buddy up with a friend or a peer and brainstorm new ideas, goals and business areas together. We personally find that working everything out on paper first is more powerful – a huge piece of paper, with a thick marker pen, making the actions and process bold and clear. We then transfer the data to an app so we can refer to it at any time.

MIND MAPPING IS ALSO AN ACCOUNTABILITY PROCESS. After you have reached a goal, look back to see if you took all the steps you needed to. If you did and you were successful, you will know how to repeat that process to get to a similar goal. You might find out that you skipped a step last time, so you can take that step out. But if you did use every step to get to the end goal, don't change the process – do it all again to achieve the same result. If the process breaks down, if you don't reach your goal, go back to your mind map to see what you were doing differently last time and what you need to add or change next time.

When we've helped other people to learn this process, we have never received any negative feedback. It's not an intrusive process – it's an EXPLOSIVE way of identifying the most beneficial ways to move forward, and making new areas and all the required actions crystal clear in your mind.

EDUCATE YOURSELF

There is no denying that childhood education forms the foundation for anyone's development and success. Whether you left school at 15 or stayed in education until you got a PhD in rocket science, once you start running your own business, it's likely you won't feel you need any more education. Think again.

WHATEVER TYPE OF BUSINESS YOU'RE RUNNING, IT WILL ALWAYS HELP YOU TO LEARN MORE. But here's the good news: unlike school or university, you never need to learn anything you don't want to, and you don't need to take exams and gain qualifications. There is an endless supply of enriching material available to everyone – stuff that will change the way you think and help you to keep improving and developing yourself and your product or service. A load of it is even free – Google anything you're interested in to find websites and blogs, and there are TED talks on just about any subject, most of which are by charismatic and talented experts. If you don't know where to start, here are some books we highly recommend:

- *The Ten Times Rule: The Only Difference Between Success and Failure*, Grant Cardone
- *Winning Ugly*, Brad Gilbert and Steve Jamison
- *The Big Leap*, Gay Hendricks
- *Ask and it is Given*, Esther and Jerry Hicks

- *The Millionaire Booklet*, Grant Cardone
- *The Go-Giver and The Go-Giver Leader*, Bob Burg and John David Mann
- *The Fred Factor*, Mark Sanborn
- *The Alchemist*, Paulo Coelho
- *The Miracle Morning*, Hal Elrod
- *Be Obsessed or Be Average*, Grant Cardone
- *Pitch Anything*, Oren Klaff
- *How to Persuade People Who Don't Want to Be Persuaded*, Joel Bauer and Mark Levy
- *Gravitational Marketing: The Science of Attracting Customers*, Jimmy Vee, Travis Miller and Joel Bauer
- *The Best of Les Brown Audio Collection*, Les Brown
- *The Magic of Thinking Big*, David J Schwartz
- *The 5 Second Rule*, Mel Robbins

Books on personal development are enjoyable and allow you to concentrate your thoughts better on whatever else you are doing during the day. Educating yourself in something new can only have positive effects, even if it's just a break from the norm or learning about an area of your business where you need to make progress. If you don't understand anything, for example Facebook or Twitter, do a bit of work on it – you might be surprised by how easy it can be and you might even develop a new passion.

MAKE NOTES

We've been surprised, over all the years we have delivered training and talks, by how few people make notes. We now provide branded notebooks and pens and actively tell people when they need to write something down. MAKING NOTES CEMENTS IDEAS IN YOUR MIND. No matter how important you consider a hundred points when you're hearing them, 30 minutes after the presentation you will remember only a few. Just as important as making notes is to keep referring to them, so that you can take the actions required to benefit from the advice you thought was so powerful when you first heard it.

Get into the habit as well of making notes whenever you think of something new – you can come up with the best ideas when you're doing something completely different. Use a dictaphone or your phone voice recorder if it's hard to keep a notebook to hand. Get in the habit of reviewing your notes and recordings – it can be as powerful as reading a personal-development book.

DEFINE YOUR MARKET

No matter what product or service you are providing, you have probably already learned which types of clients are of most value to you and how to filter out some of the others. Nine times out of ten, defining your ideal customer and adapting your product or service to suit their preferences and requirements leads to MORE business, not less.

Time and again, we see clear examples of business owners seeing their business levels multiply, as a direct result of *narrowing* their target market. And those business owners soon become happier and more confident, knowing that their product or service is perfect for the people they're selling to.

FILTER OUT NON-STARTERS

We often get asked how we focus on the right people at a wedding fair, which is essentially a trade show for wedding suppliers. Whenever you are at a trade show or similar, it is important you learn how to maximise your success with the people who are most likely to give you business.

Look for the ways you can find out, at the start of any conversation, how likely it is that someone will place a booking or make a purchase. Ours is quite easy: 'Hi guys, when are you getting married?'. If they haven't yet got a date for their wedding, we'll reduce our time with them and give them a brochure to take away. If a couple already has a date, it is worth making the effort to get them to make a booking that day. If we stop to give other people lots of time, we'll be missing a chance to talk to the ones who are ready to book.

Some time ago, Spencer started trying a new tactic, which delivers IMPRESSIVE RESULTS. If someone gives him two possible dates they're thinking of, he allows them to book both dates. He takes one deposit, then as soon as they're ready to confirm, he frees up the other date in his diary. In the meantime, if he can fill either of the dates, he gets back in contact with first client to say he has had to let one of those dates go. He'll sell every free date in his diary to one client, if that's what it's going to take to secure that booking.

WHEN TO ARRANGE MEETINGS

People often ask us how important it is to arrange a meeting with a prospective client. There are three main things to consider here:

1. **Cost vs certainty** – you want to give any prospect a good impression of your flexibility and collaboration, but if you bend over backwards too far, you'll fall over. There's no point wasting half a day and a train fare to meet up with someone who might only book a £100 job or place a small order, especially if it's not very certain they'll sign up at all. Don't feel bad in turning down their request for a meeting if your time can be spent more valuably elsewhere – simply explain tactfully that it will be just as beneficial to talk on the phone or via Skype at this stage.

2. **Future potential** – if you're creating a connection with someone whose company is likely to place future orders, or with someone who has good connections with other valuable businesses, place more importance on meeting with them now, even if you're unlikely to get an order that day. You can then deliver an impactful experience to highlight all your potential benefits to their company or to other people they know. Don't forget the importance of non-stop networking and connectivity!

3. **Will they come to you?** Even if you know that a meeting will be valuable, this is an ultimate solution to work towards. Suppliers and clients are always willing to go out of their way to meet with people who are sufficiently successful and important in their line of business. If

or when you are confident (or can act confidently) enough to persuade any prospect to come to you, you'll not only save time and money, you will have elevated their level of respect and belief in you. That in turn will increase the chances of them making a booking or placing an order.

Lee has become especially good at the last point. Unless it's for a massive contract or a very important client, if someone isn't willing to make the journey to him, he's not interested in the booking. After all, it's almost certain he'll be able to fill that date, whilst still saving himself the time and expense of a meeting far from where he's based. Then any prospect who is willing to make the extra effort is guaranteed to be more serious about the business – NINE TIMES OUT OF TEN, HE'S GOT THE BOOKING BEFORE THEY EVEN ARRIVE.

WHEN TO TAKE PAYMENT

When to demand payment can depend on the industry you work in, and you might already have very clear rules, with rock-solid terms and conditions around your invoices. This is less of a problem with products, although some business clients do still ask to make payment after delivery.

Please bear in mind that one of the biggest causes of business failure is a problem with cashflow, which is usually due to late payment of invoices. No matter what type of business you run, it is essential to be strict and upfront about payment terms. Unless you're providing a very high-end product or service and are willing to offer special payment terms, you should always work towards receiving full payment on the day you deliver. In the service industry, there is an extra advantage to requesting payment before the day you provide the service. Suddenly asking someone for a payment just after you've finished your work can have a negative impact at the end of an otherwise positive experience.

In his first session with a therapist, at the end of the 50 minutes, the therapist asked Spencer for payment, then she started rifling through her handbag for a tenner to give him his change. Spencer says that annihilated any good feelings and positive effects of the session. He had enjoyed the session and found benefit from talking to the therapist. When she asked for her money, he said – in his usual direct manner – 'YOU'VE JUST MADE IT ABOUT BUSINESS, NOT ABOUT CARING ABOUT ME'. The therapist was really surprised, saying that was the first time anyone had said that. Spencer's rationale is that, say if he went and slept with a prostitute, then at the end she asked for money, turning it into a business transaction would immediately ruin an otherwise enjoyable and sensual experience. It would be far better, in both these cases, to ask for the money in advance. Spencer told his therapist that from that point on he would prefer to pay up front, and he swears it increased the effectiveness of subsequent therapy sessions. This example brings us to the TABOO so many people feel about seeking therapy. Nearly all of the most successful businesspeople in the world have therapy to improve their mental wellbeing and personal success levels. (We have no idea if they visit prostitutes – Spencer's example was purely hypothetical.) Please don't feel bad about seeking therapy if you ever want to clear your head or improve your mindset – THERE IS NOTHING WRONG WITH IT.

We also both firmly believe that it's better not to ask for too much of the final payment too far ahead. Taking a minimal deposit for standard bookings has four advantages:

1. The deposit is small enough for people not to try and claim it back if they cancel. A deposit is exactly that, after all – a non-refundable payment for placing the booking. You will have spent time converting the sale, as well as potentially turning down another booking for that date. That said, if someone kicks up a fuss, let it go. Fighting over £100 isn't worth the grief and time involved, and you risk bad publicity if you're dealing with somebody who is likely to be unreasonable.

2. The bulk of the payment will come in the correct financial year, i.e. when you're providing the service.

3. If you receive full payment two years ahead of a booking, by the time you are delivering your service it will feel like you're doing it for nothing, which will reduce your levels of dedication, motivation and energy.

4. If you take full payment up front then the client cancels, paying most or all of it back at a later date will be difficult and/or unpleasant.

It can often happen, especially with corporate clients, that people will try to set their own payment terms, say 30–60 days after you've provided a product or service. We highly recommend that you make every effort to resist that, as long as you're not endangering a big contract or your own business. Take any steps required in order to make your contract watertight, to ensure that any company sticks to your payment terms.

EXPENSE VERSUS INCOME

Remember that the problem is never about what things cost, especially if you are considering a positive investment in something for your business. The problem lies purely with your income. If something is outside your budget, don't think about how you are unable to invest in it, just find ways to earn more so that you *can* afford it. You can always find ways to bring in more money. This is another **MAGIC VORTEX** – when you find yourself, a few months down the line, having afforded what you wanted, you will realise it is possible and keep looking for other new ways to increase your income in order to make bigger investments.

KEEPING ON TOP OF CALLS AND EMAILS

You might have already gathered that we are both proactive people. We like to ensure we efficiently manage our time and anything to do with our businesses, to leave plenty of time for other important activities.

You probably already know how stressful it can feel to have 50 unread emails in your inbox and a long list of people you need to call. Multiply that by 100, and you will have an idea of how the same situation feels to Lee! As soon as he wakes up in the morning, he feels physically stressed-out and unable to focus on anything big until he's on top of all his calls and emails. This might sound a little extreme, but it can also be inspirational in how you can learn to keep on top of everything. Lee's got to be doing something right, with the phenomenal number of valuable contacts he has. As we outlined in Chapter 4, Lee stores standard responses in notes on his phone, to copy and paste into emails. He goes out of his way to connect with everyone he can at any company, venue or event. He collects their business cards, and makes some contact with each person that same day. Then, in addition to not delaying on any call he needs to make, he makes time whenever he can to call other people, to establish a connection, arrange a meeting or exchange business ideas.

We are both 100% proactive in chasing up gig enquiries. We set timelines for our calls, then keep calling at specific times until we receive a firm response. We follow up on every corporate event we perform at to find out if they are doing the same again the next year. We make a huge effort to keep in contact with previous clients, to make them feel valued and encourage them to book again with us. We KNOW this approach gives our businesses a massive boost, securing bookings we wouldn't otherwise have achieved. Once you get in the disciplined habit of applying this sort of approach to any type of communication with your customers, IT DOESN'T NEED TO FEEL LIKE A CHORE – it's just another thing you include in your day-to-day planning in order to stay successful.

There are huge variances across different industries and businesses in the most efficient ways of managing communication with clients. There are ways to find out, say, how quickly you need to respond to prospects' emails in order to achieve maximum conversion rates. At the end of this chapter, you will read about the super-efficient ways that Dr Shotter uses to manage customer communications, which may well prove more beneficial to you, depending on your type of business and the volume of emails and calls you receive.

SOCIAL MEDIA
HAVE YOU EVER EARNED £1K IN 30 SECONDS?
It really is possible. Within half a minute, using an existing testimonial or a photo with a couple of lines of text, you can create and post a free ad on Facebook, which can generate multiple enquiries or orders.

If you can place an ad within 30 seconds, how many other things can you think of to do like that? There are hundreds of ways to advertise on social media, and loads of them are free. The potential is phenomenal. Facebook is great for both of us. We have established a large number of vital contacts, each of whom sees all our updates and developments, which raises our brand awareness. We post regularly and accept bookings. We have set up and joined closed groups, where industry specialists share incredibly powerful strategies. The business we gain from social media makes up a significant part of our income.

If you're not yet fully familiar with the types of social media best suited to your type of business, we strenuously recommend that you find ways either to learn everything you need to, or to find a company that can manage your social media campaigns for you. If you are already on social media, make the time and effort to be proactive with it, and you will experience INCREDIBLE RESULTS.

There are people who will always complain. 'Social media is killing me', 'You're losing your ability to get out in front of people', 'You're hiding behind your online profile', 'You post too much'. Comments that nearly always only reflect some sort of negativity or jealousy from their side about what you are doing. Ignore it, keep increasing your activity, and enjoy the results. Once you get familiar with how to get the most from social media, it is quick and easy to keep your activity levels up, and it becomes enjoyable to learn about new developments in how you can increase your visibility and your income. SOMETHING YOU ENJOY AND MAKE LOTS OF MONEY DOING – WHAT COULD BE BETTER THAN THAT?

MONSTER TIPS

When you're ready to try for a Monster, i.e. a job for which you will earn considerably more than you normally would, remember this: start high in your negotiations. You are extremely unlikely to end up with much less than where you started. For example, if you start off at £5,000, if the client gets you down to £3,850, they'll think they've got a result and you'll still be very happy with the price you settled on.

Here's another tip: don't rush the Monster process. You have to gain sufficient confidence first, in your product or service, and in the improvements you can make in order to perform better and charge significantly more. It will also make a massive difference to the confidence you exude when pitching for a Monster if you are in a financially secure position. Wait until you have exceeded your goals for the year ahead, and you will be confident enough to ask outright for a higher price.

OUTSOURCING

If you know you should be doing something but a) you hate doing it or b) you struggle to do it well, LETITGO. Your time is more valuable doing what you do best, not getting frustrated by the time you are wasting trying to master other things. It's not just work stuff you can outsource – if you know you're going to earn more in a week than it would cost to pay a decorator to paint your house, let them get on with it, while you get on with your work.

That's our potted version. Dr Sophie Shotter has considerably more experience with outsourcing, which she has kindly agreed to share with us. Sophie has also developed a robust system for managing the communication side of her businesses. While we don't need to be as strict with our time, due to the different types and volumes of emails and calls we receive, we have already made improvements thanks to her advice. As we said at the start of this chapter, there will always be new things you can (and need to) do, in order to keep improving and increasing your business; we hope you'll gain similar inspiration here from us and from Dr Shotter. We'll entrust the rest of this chapter to her, before we move on to helping you to gain massive motivation to succeed.

Sophie is a fully trained medical doctor. After qualifying, she worked for six years as an anaesthetist in the NHS, before setting up her own business. While the treatments she provides deliver outstanding results, the real strength of her businesses comes from her dedication and natural business acumen. We are grateful that she made time in her very busy schedule to share some of her techniques with us.

INTERVIEW WITH DR SOPHIE SHOTTER
THE ILLUMINATE SKIN CLINICS, KENT

What made you decide to start your own business?

While I was working in the NHS, I started feeling obliged to accept overtime and ended up working the most ridiculous hours for little reward. So I set up my business initially as a sideline, partly so that I had another responsibility and a reason to say no to the other demands that were being put on me. And I fell in love with it. Not just the field – aesthetic medicine, and what I could do for people – but the entrepreneurial side. It just feels like that side of me keeps flourishing and growing. I have new ideas all the time; it's now more about filtering out what's worth doing and what isn't. It's not always been easy – I am a doctor, and I've learnt all this as I've gone along. There's so much I don't know, and I can't say it hasn't been a tough learning curve, but I love every minute.

Could you tell us about how you manage your emails?

My business is different from yours. If I understand it correctly, you don't have many overheads, so you can afford to create time where you're not necessarily bringing in revenue, to deal with your emails. But if I have to check my emails throughout the day, it's distracting and stops me from getting other things done. With my business plans and the growth I want to achieve, I need to stay focused on tasks and jobs that need to be completed. If I'm constantly getting notifications that I've got mail, it's distracting. I now have a PA who sends me a summary of my inbox twice a day, for me to respond to the ones I need to or tell her the response required.

Before I could afford a PA, I decided on three set times every day – in the morning, at lunchtime and in the evening – to look at my emails. I also turned off the automatic mail notifications on my MacBook, so my inbox just didn't interfere with my day-to-day life. I guess the only downside to that is if you don't have anyone to help you with sales enquiries. In the aesthetic industry, the gold standard is for sales calls to be responded to within a short time; it's been shown that if you get an enquiry and you respond within an hour, your chance of converting is very decent. But they drop off significantly even after five minutes – the moment you leave it over an hour, your chances of that person coming into your clinic are very low. Basically, if someone has Googled a number of clinics and sent a few emails, the one that gets back to them first is the one they're most likely to go with. That's why I have set very clear targets within our working hours.

I got the statistical information from a brilliant business consultant I've worked with, but anyone can find the same sort of information out if they're willing to pay for it and/or spend time researching their own market. If it's a smaller business in a less generic industry, people will be able to work it out for themselves, based on their own response times and conversion rates. They then need to build a structure around that information and create some targets to reach their own gold standard. It's all industry-specific, and I expect in some industries you won't lose business if you reply, say, within four hours. If your ideal response time is short, it can be a trickier balance to strike, but if you can't afford someone in-house, you can still outsource to a virtual assistant. The way I see it, the tough part as a business owner is reaching the ideal balance, between working *in* your business and working *on* your business.

A lot of people use programs to generate auto-responders, but what works for us is an out-of-office response, with an automatic response that gets sent out to every sales enquiry. It says something like 'Thank you so much for getting in touch, these are our normal working hours. If you contact us within this time, we will get back to you within X amount of time. If it's outside those hours, we'll get back to you as soon as we're back in the clinic.' It's a touch point for the prospect and something anyone can do with their email program.

I also have a bank of templates for responding to emails, which are a constant work in progress. They're warm and carry through our brand values in how we want to come across. We've put a lot of work into them, giving people enough information and not too much, making sure we get across to people how warm and friendly we are, how we're professional but aren't going to be worried about how their grammar is. It's incredibly easy to set up – every email program has signatures, so we have 25 different signatures. Then they get a prompt and professional response. It's a really easy and effective way to maintain your standards.

The only thing that would be more urgent would be a patient who had a complication from a treatment. In work hours, that inbox is constantly monitored, and we have an out-of-hours mobile in case there is a very urgent problem, but I can honestly say that I've never had that happen.

If friends try to WhatsApp me, say, they will get a much slower response; I just have to tactfully ask them to contact me in another way next time, so they'll get a quicker response. I just firmly believe that we all need boundaries and switch-off time.

Do you take the same approach with phone calls?

From the word go, I took the decision that I wouldn't take any business phone calls. In all honesty, my phone stays on divert unless I am expecting a specific call. If someone wants to get hold of me, they can leave me a message and I'll respond when I have time.

My phone is always on silent. Even if I get a text message, I don't know about it until I decide to look at my phone, and that's only when I am on a break. So all that communication doesn't interfere with what I'm trying to get done. That may be seeing a patient – the money-bringing side of my business – or it could be if I have a deadline for another job I need to get done, where I want to keep my headspace clear. For the phone, I outsource to a call-answering service, so I know that my calls are always being answered. If someone needs to get hold of me personally, I will respond to their voicemail as soon as I have time.

What are your experiences of outsourcing?

Say for you, no one else could go and do your performances, but someone else could do your emails. With a lot of small business owners, when we're at the stage when we're growing, the thing that limits us is actually ourselves. We try to keep control of too many things and we're afraid of letting things go, so we try to be the Jack of all trades, but we can't do all of it.

In my case, I'm a doctor – the thing I'm best at is my treatments. There are other things I do well, which I can do, but the question is whether I *should* be doing them, when there are people out there that can do them better. Wherever I think there is someone who has more expertise at something, I outsource it. I have very tight cost controls as well, so I'm always aware of that, but I just try and think about what is most efficient in a business sense.

Someone else does my digital marketing, for example – that's bringing me more business in, therefore my value is in my business, doing what I'm best at and bringing in the money to pay for the digital marketing. When I started out, I tried to do my own digital marketing; I paid for programs, learnt all about it, implemented it, and I was still achieving really low outcomes. There are some things that we all try to do in our business that we would be better off outsourcing. Sometimes it takes a leap of faith and an investment, but it can bring you a better amount of money back.

I have had things that haven't worked out along the way. I had the same phone answering service for three years; they were great at first, but as they grew bigger they couldn't maintain the same standards. I soon found that my standard of customer service wasn't being maintained by them. The difficulty there was proving things. Whenever I've had to complain, unless I could provide concrete proof, it's been denied. Getting other people to take accountability for their actions can be hard, but you mustn't be afraid to ask questions. My first virtual PA was lovely, but she was a one-man band. She was going through personal difficulties, and that was making my life more difficult instead of easier. Maybe that's what I've had to learn most, to lead with my head not my heart – intrinsically, you like people and want to support them, but you have to make certain decisions to protect your business. You've got to make sure you retain a distance. By nature, I'm someone who nurtures people. When I've had those experiences where people haven't delivered, I've always handled it in a nice way. If you part ways with a service provider, someone you have got to know, you don't actually need to tell them all the reasons why you're not satisfied.

My biggest advice is to measure. Get word-of-mouth recommendations whenever you can. If you can't, get comparable quotes, find out what people are offering in their different packages and what their USPs are, then measure. Keep on top of the situation and let them know early on if you have any doubts – you're just making it clear that you're monitoring the situation. If you're spending money, it's just got to work for you.

We go into this thinking that everyone's like us – driven, keen to keep their customers happy and provide as good a level of service as we are. When you realise that's not always true, it does make you more cynical and it teaches you how you need to do careful research. And don't always go for the cheapest provider. I'm now in the process of having a new website built – it's costing me five times as much as last time, but I'm now in the position where I can spend that money, and I know it's worth it.

What are the main benefits you see from all your approaches to managing communication and outsourcing?

I honestly believe that managing time is one of the biggest challenges for any small business owner. I think we all worry that if we don't respond to something straight away, we're going to be deemed unprofessional or rude. Actually, that's not the case. We all put so much pressure on ourselves, but you don't get paid for answering an email. Your time is expensive, because your time is where the money is. I know what my time costs, and I have jobs in my personal and business life that I categorise by judging what they effectively cost per hour to complete. I now won't touch anything under a £100 per hour job. Don't get me wrong – I'll clean toilets if I need to do it – but this is about prioritising my time in the most efficient and business-effective ways possible.

Another thing I do, when I bring people in and outsource, is to make sure I don't remain ignorant. I make sure I learn from them. When I hire a call-answering company, I have a very clear idea of how I want them to answer the phone and what standard I expect of them. Then if something goes wrong, I can go back to what I have required them to do. If you have an understanding of what you're outsourcing, rather than blindly trusting them, I think you're far more likely to get a satisfactory relationship. It also means that if you have a time between contracts with those people, you have an idea of how to do it yourself for as long as you need to.

You might find yourself overwhelmed with guilt about how quickly you respond to contacts – from friends, customers, anyone – but why should you feel guilty if you're doing what's right for you? You're not being selfish; you're just doing things in the way that works best for you. Some of my friends sometimes have to wait longer for a response than I might like, but they all get it – they all know what my life's like and they don't make me feel bad about it. Friends understand and, ultimately, I'm sure they respect you more for it.

From a work perspective, people get an auto-response, then an email from my PA to say she's checking on something for them and that she'll get back to them, then they don't feel like they're being ignored.

Where can you see yourself going from here?

I currently have two businesses, and I expect that number will grow in the next year. I currently have a clinic and also a consulting business, through which I speak and do advisory board and key opinion leader work, and also consultancy work, plus some consulting for other clinics as well. The consulting business probably won't grow much from where it's at, but I'm happy with that; the clinic is growing very, very quickly at the moment.

I deliver non-invasive treatments – I'm not a surgeon by background and I didn't want to go down the surgery route. While there are some people that do need surgery, I expect that in a few years you will find that the market is almost all for needles rather than knives. The things we can already achieve without surgery are incredible, and most people don't want dramatic results with significant downtime and huge costs. They prefer to be subtle and stay looking natural.

I work incredibly long hours sometimes but I 100% enjoy what I do. And I can do it mainly thanks to the structures I've put in place that make everything manageable.

CHAPTER 9
Motivation to succeed

After three hefty chapters, on mastering selling, managing your money and constantly improving your business, we're going to give you a short, relaxing break. Don't relax too much – this chapter's going to challenge your status quo and make you realise just how much motivation you need to stay successful. We'll tell you how to get there, though.

There are two quotes, from successful businessmen, that really sum this chapter up:

The critical ingredient is getting off your butt and doing something. It's as simple as that. A lot of people have ideas, but there are few who decide to do something about them now. Not tomorrow. Not next week. But today. The true entrepreneur is a doer, not a dreamer.
Nolan Bushnell

I'm convinced that about half of what separates the successful entrepreneurs from the non-successful ones is pure perseverance.
Steve Jobs

Those quotes make it sound very simple, but there's no question that it can be hard to keep up your motivation levels at any stage of running your own business. When you first make the decision to leave your day job, one of the first challenges you'll face is no longer having a boss or a team of colleagues to motivate you. There will be times when you experience setbacks that will reduce your personal drive, which might sometimes make you question if you've done the right thing. And even when your business is well established, lack of motivation can dilute your confidence in keeping on top of day-to-day admin or aiming for a new goal.

Let's turn all this around. Don't focus on why you might feel unmotivated, and don't beat yourself up whenever you do. Here are the positive ways we have found to maintain our own levels of motivation, even when the going gets tough.

FIND A MENTOR

A business mentor's experience and business advice will be invaluable. They'll help you look at everything from a fresh perspective whenever you're feeling bogged down by new challenges. Your mentor will help you establish new contacts, especially because they will have your best interests at heart and be keen to help you develop your own network and client base. They will give you encouragement and help you increase your confidence. All in all, they will boost your levels of motivation.

FINDING A MENTOR CAN BE EASIER THAN YOU THINK. It could be simply a matter of asking someone you already know, whose approaches inspire you. You could start off subtly, by asking someone who is successful in your line of business if they would be willing to share some advice. If they say 'no', just ask someone else – you'll be surprised by how quickly you'll find that really positive and open person who is flattered to be asked and more than happy to help you.

It's important to remember that this isn't a one-way relationship – people who have been successful in business enjoy positive repercussions from helping others up. We'll tell you about that in Chapter 10, for whenever you're ready to be a mentor for someone else. For now, don't let yourself feel any negativity about finding a mentor and asking for advice – it is mutually beneficial, and the impact on you and your business will be enormous. ULTIMATELY, PEOPLE WILL RESPECT YOU MORE FOR PROFITING FROM SOMEONE ELSE'S EXPERIENCE THAN FOR MAKING SLOWER PROGRESS ON YOUR OWN.

SEEK INSPIRATION

Get in the habit of watching anyone else – in any type of business – who is successful at what they are doing. This has to be one of the quickest and easiest ways to achieve better results. Read blogs, watch other people's activity on social media, find out about their clients and their suppliers . . . do whatever you can to find out how they got to where they are now. If you can, watch the people who are right at the top – they're the ones that are doing it best. If it's difficult to find out about them, if you need to make a lot of effort to seek them out, then they're doing something really right.

Listen to talks by motivational speakers. Or go back to the parts you highlighted in personal-development books that gave you motivation when you were reading them. Even just looking up some quotes from successful people can be enough to remind you to keep going and keep taking action.

When Lee was first introduced to the teams of clients and colleagues of Trevor Liley (his business mentor), he soon learned about the six-figure and seven-figure deals they were discussing, and their off-the-scale budgets. Lee couldn't believe what he was hearing – it was in a different league from anything he was used to – but those numbers were just normal for that set of people. Lee's levels of self-motivation took an immediate boost. Spending time with successful people will have a massive impact on your motivation levels. When you find out how many of those people started from nothing, you'll realise how you could do the same. Experiencing how much other people are earning and are willing to spend will increase your own aspirations and goals.

If you're lucky enough to have formed a Buddy Up relationship, focus on boosting each other's motivation levels. It can be easiest to vent frustrations with a person you work closely with, knowing they'll understand where you're coming from. But negative conversations will make you the negative person we recommended you cut out of your life. KEEP FOCUSING ON INCREASING EACH OTHER'S MOTIVATION LEVELS – THE PAY-OFF WILL BE MUTUALLY REWARDING.

DON'T PROCRASTINATE

When you're lacking motivation, it can be very easy to keep finding reasons for why you don't need to be taking action, even though you know deep-down what you should be doing and why. You probably already know that when you do finally get going, your motivation increases, making it easier and easier to get on with everything else. This is a black-and-white reminder from us: DON'TPROCRASTINATE. Whenever you would normally think 'I'll do that tomorrow', force yourself not even to consider saying that – just get on with the task straight away.

Make sure you achieve something new the moment you put this book down. Start thinking about it now, write it down, and do it as soon as you take a break from reading. Go out there tomorrow and start talking to people. Create mind maps, set new goals, work on your WIDIFY, look for a business mentor . . . start working on any of the things we have recommended in this book, and you will feel your motivation start to grow. Act on all of them, and you'll soon be wondering how you ever felt unmotivated. Back to the **MAGIC VORTEX**: once you're taking action, enjoying the repercussions and achieving fantastic results, your motivation levels will be sky-high. The only thing stopping you from getting there is procrastination. If you put in, you get back – it's as simple as that. Take massive amounts of action as soon as you possibly can, and you won't even need to come back to this chapter.

KEEP DOING WHAT WORKS

Hands up – this is something we also need to work on. When you have found something that works, you HAVE to keep doing it. It's like watering a plant to make it grow and keep it flowering. WHEN YOU STOP WATERING IT, THE PLANT WILL DIE AND YOU'LL HAVE TO START OVER AGAIN.

There have been times when we have taken advice or developed our own new way of tackling a challenge. We've invested time and effort in learning the new approach and soon started enjoying the results.

We might have been so pleased with the outcome that we told other people about it, recommending they do the same. Then suddenly – in part because we were feeling more successful and things seemed easier – we've taken our foot off the gas and got out of the habit of applying that approach. Any time we've done that, it's taken some time before we have re-evaluated and realised exactly why our results have taken a hit. Then we've had to invest more time and effort to adopt that new discipline into our everyday routine.

We're getting better at predicting and avoiding this kind of setback, at training our brains to keep in the right mindset and to stick with any approach that delivers results. We hope this forewarning will help you to get there more quickly. You just need to make sure you stick to successful habits, without stopping, and you'll maintain your results and your motivation.

APPRECIATE YOURSELF

Whenever you're lacking in motivation, it's almost inevitable that your inner critic will be having a field day. 'You'll never get everything done. You didn't get that order you wanted. Is this ever going to work?'

SELF-APPRECIATION AND SELF-MOTIVATION GO HAND IN HAND. If your inner critic is digging away at your self-confidence, take some time – however busy you are – to stop and look at where you are and what you have already achieved. If you're doing something you love, it's no doubt considerably more enjoyable than your last job. Try and remember the point where, the minute you got out of bed, you felt that full-on dread at the prospect of going to work. You have now become one of the lucky ones – maybe less than 10% of the population – who actually enjoy their careers. You're experiencing some stress and setbacks, but didn't you have that in your last job? And how much better is it being your own boss, earning only for yourself and your family, and deciding on when you want to be where?

Write down every milestone you have already reached in establishing your business. Think of each goal you've achieved and remember how good you felt at that time. Consider all the new things you have learned and the courage it took to start working for yourself. Remind yourself of your desire to achieve and how you are certain you are going to make this work.

You get the picture – focus on the positive, appreciate how far you have come, and decide that you're going to be more motivated tomorrow. Then write the list of actions you are going to take. And don't procrastinate.

EXTERNAL INFLUENCES

There will be habits you have found (or can find) that take up little or no time, which can increase your positivity. You may have a favourite type of music, one that boosts your mood or makes you remember a positive time. Taking a walk or going to the gym can clear your head and help you see everything from a fresher perspective. Ten minutes listening to a YouTube clip on self-confidence or a mindfulness meditation can reduce the time taken on a challenging task and increase the outcome. The list is endless.

Keep looking for ways to improve your mood and your motivation levels, then make them part of your everyday routine.

REMEMBER THE MONEY

Again, you've got to define your success on your own terms. But if, like the majority of people, you would like to increase your income, focusing on the financial rewards might be enough to fuel your motivation. Remember to think of your income over the course of the year, i.e. that not every month has to be a bumper month. Don't feel down if you don't reach your monthly target; try and see it as extra motivation to achieve more in order to reach your annual target.

Be strict on yourself about thinking positively around the reasons you want to achieve a certain level of income – that you are providing for your family, or you are saving for a new car or a new house. Keep those goals in mind and you'll feel passion and an emotional connection to what you are aiming for. Hey, you'll have WIDIFYed yourself.

Here's a quick list of three additional points that count towards increasing your motivation levels.

- **Start with a routine.** Starting each morning with a routine is a great way to banish early-morning lack of motivation. Get up at a set time then do something that increases your energy and/ or confidence levels, like going for a run or doing ten minutes of meditation. Then write a plan of the tasks you are going to achieve that day . . . and get going. You will be amazed by the difference to your motivation levels for the whole day.

- **Set rewards.** We are hard-wired to perform better when there is an extra incentive. Set yourself rewards and make sure you never cheat by collecting a reward early. We're talking here about small rewards for victories throughout the day – a coffee break when you've cleared your inbox; or a favourite snack on your desk, which you're only allowed to eat after you've arranged three new meetings.

- **Start off on the right foot.** On your way to a meeting, listen to something positive – a motivational speaker, a self-confidence meditation or your favourite upbeat music. You'll start the meeting substantially more motivated than if you just sat watching dreary commuters on the train or in the cars around you, and we bet you anything you'll gain better results from that meeting.

PERSEVERE, NO MATTER WHAT

We'll finish this chapter with the all-important extra factor in your motivation to succeed: PERSEVERANCE. You've got to maintain your activity levels and stay positive, constantly. Even in bad situations, if you stay positive, you will stay strong and continue to grow.

You won't achieve your end goal today or tomorrow, but you need to keep believing that it *will* happen. As long as you persist in churning out new ideas and taking action in any way you can, you will get closer and closer to your goals. Things will keep happening on your journey that will make you automatically raise your game. You'll find your mindset developing, you'll keep thinking bigger, and positive things will keep happening. Your motivation levels will allow you to take action in all the areas of this book – improving your mindset, networking, setting yourself goals, selling successfully and keeping on top of your numbers and the management of your business. At the same time, your negativity will decrease and you will find it easier and easier to stay focused and motivated.

You've got to look at the long game as well – the bigger picture – and remain determined to grow ... and grow ... and grow. We both *know* that we will continue to improve in business and achieve higher goals. WE WILL NEVER STOP STRIVING TO ACHIEVE MORE. We're going to enjoy the challenges and the setbacks, knowing that they are an inevitable part of the journey. We're going to keep pushing ourselves out of our comfort zones, to progress to each next stage. If we don't, we'll just stay at the levels of business and income we have now. You need to keep moving on, no matter what.

If you're sitting waiting for the phone to ring, it won't. If you want a better quality of life, then do things in bigger quantity in life. Ensure you do everything you need to in order to reach any goal you're working towards. **All you have to do to make things happen is to keep thinking positively and taking action, then everything else will fall into place.**

Lee has recently helped a musician, Roxy, to identify new and more profitable areas of business. Roxy has since told Lee that she has experienced a huge improvement in her motivation levels since their meeting, and she was very happy to give the following feedback to our copy-editor.

FEEDBACK FROM ROXY SEARLE – MUSICIAN

I met Lee quite a few years ago now, but I didn't realise that he helped people in business until recently, when I was in a bit of a stagnant stage in my business. I just didn't really know how to progress – I play guitar and I sing, and I fixated on pub gigs and weddings. Then I caught up with Lee, and he asked if I wanted to meet up with him for a coffee and have a chat about business.

In the music business, it's very hard to find people who want to support what you do, rather than see you as competition or a threat. Lee is completely the opposite of that – he changed my perception on everything.

Lee went through all the steps I could take and made it so simple for me. I walked away thinking, 'That is just so straightforward and so *right*; I only needed someone to point it out to me.' I needed that guidance and inspiration, and I needed the encouragement to do it. It's easy to sit there and say, 'I'd like to do this' or 'I'd like to be able to do that', but Lee has this way of making you think, 'I *can* do this' or 'I'm *going* to do that'. I got home and filled up half a notebook, full of ideas. I'm dyslexic, so I find it hard to write, which is why I've gone into music, to express myself in a creative way. But I was writing and writing and writing . . . I felt like I had a clear direction of what I wanted to achieve and where I wanted to go. Everything fell into place for me.

I started in music when I was nine years old, in musicals like *Mary Poppins* and *Chitty Chitty Bang Bang* in the West End. From that time, my mum was my 'driver', getting my gigs for me. Over the last year or so, I've taken it over for myself but, although I was getting all these gigs, I didn't feel that I was going anywhere. But Lee has really pushed me. I'm writing a lot more, which is amazing for me – I have a huge passion for writing music. I've been able to do a lot more with my guitar, learning new songs and having the confidence to approach people I wouldn't have before.

I'm now getting into corporate events, for companies like Mercedes, Ocado and Caterham Cars. It started with someone I know at Ocado – I simply asked if they had any events coming up and whether I could put my card forward for those. I wouldn't have done that before talking to Lee.

Lee told me about a 'Monster' – a really big job to aim for – and he's given me so much inspiration to get myself my own Monsters. It's changed my whole mindset. It's massively pushed me to want to catch the big fish. If I concentrate on the big fish, I don't feel as much pressure to get the small fish. I see the music business as a pond. I put my rod out there, and if I get a big fish that's amazing, but when I only get a small fish, that's still great – it's still a fish!

The STEP System is like a tool in your tool belt, or maybe it's more than that – it's the belt that you can put the tools into. Mind maps are massively important – my other half and I really look forward to doing them together. He puts them on an app, but I prefer to see them on paper. I'm really creative with it, and I mind map most days. As soon as something comes into my head, I think about how I can explore the potential of that idea. It helps me to be more creative and also more settled in my own mind, so there's not so much stuff floating around in your brain. You're able to get it down and then let your mind rest.

My motivation probably used to come from my mum. She never pushed me, but she always supported me. The older I got – I'm now 23 – the more I wanted to be independent. There was a specific turning point, where I recently did a wedding for a friend, Emma. She had asked me not to start until she had arrived at the venue, and she even cut her photograph session short because she didn't want to miss the start of my performance. That really shocked me, and as she walked in and I started to sing, her face lit up. That was everything for me – absolutely everything – I think I found myself again when I saw that. I really felt that I was doing this for a reason, other than just for myself – I was doing it to help other people as well and make other people feel happy.

That was just after I met up with Lee – he had helped with my motivation to do things like that, then the way that Emma reacted stimulated the emotions behind it. Motivation and emotions are strongly interconnected. Now my motivation just keeps growing – Lee has helped me so much with new ideas, support and guidance. He says he's not going to sugar-coat it, that it's going to be difficult, but that when you eventually do get it, it's going to be worth it. He's given me the confidence too to increase and be confident in my prices. I just wasn't as confident as I should have been in my pricing, but Lee's given me the encouragement to say 'This is the price I charge – if you don't want to pay that, there will be other people who will charge less. But you're paying for a once-in-a-lifetime experience.' Quality is so important to me – I could not turn up to a wedding and do a half-hearted performance of songs that I've chosen. I spend a lot of time with my bride and groom, to tailor the music especially for their wedding – they can decide on the speed of the songs; if they want a certain verse cut out; or if they want me to create another verse for them, to tailor it to them.

Hopefully, I'll just keep growing! Lee taught me that nothing is going to fall in my lap – if you want something, you have to go and get it. I'm hoping to make him proud, make my family proud and make myself proud. I want to become a huge success and to build an empire – that's exactly what I am aiming for. My behaviour has changed dramatically recently, and my other half and my parents are very supportive, so I know I can only go from strength to strength.

CHAPTER 10

It's not all about you

We quite often meet and help people who lack some confidence in dealing with other people. They may be naturally quite introverted or shy. They may be 100% relaxed in an informal setting but feel nervous when they talk to outsiders at a business meeting. Or they may just feel that they never really create a lasting impression on other people. If any of this is sounding familiar, we hope you will benefit from the practical advice in this chapter. And even if you're a natural people person, you will still benefit from thinking logically about new ways to approach other people in business.

We've already emphasised that business is all about people. Everything else, like investment, technology, numbers, processes and marketing, are still essential factors in the success of your business, but the decision makers are people who you need to win round.

We're not psychiatrists or pretending to be experts on this subject, but our talents and routes to success are rooted in understanding, entertaining and engaging with people, so we do feel qualified to pass on some sound advice. We're going to start with a system that will enable you to identify the type of person you are dealing with, in order to tailor your approach to them. Then we'll give you a few general tips on how you can improve your rapport-building skills. Finally, we hope to inspire you in this chapter to consider one day helping other people up, to help them to achieve what you have achieved.

TAILORING YOUR APPROACH TO OTHER PEOPLE
There have been a number of books and articles about analysing people's personalities, to fit them into a small number of types of

character, in order to understand them better and to know how best to deal with them.

While face-to-face people skills are probably the strongest asset for both of us, we have both been inspired by the benefits of defining personality types. For example, once you logically work out that the person you are dealing with is only really interested in the technical aspects and numbers of a service, you can tailor your communication and sales pitch accordingly. There's going to be no point placing most emphasis on how much fun guests will have at a corporate event, when your prospect only wants to hear about the ROI figures and the number of leads you guarantee.

The only problem we've found around this subject is the confusing number of slightly different approaches. Some sources use colours to represent the character types, others use animals. Some use descriptions like 'warriors' and 'whingers', which has to be too judgmental. Most sources distinguish four types, while others use up to 16, which feels way too complicated. Like the rest of this book, we want to keep this simple. We think it's easy to explain in a few paragraphs how to define different types of people and use that information to your advantage. We stick to four types of people, and...

WE HAD OUR OWN EUREKA MOMENT

...we came up with the ideal positive and easy-to-remember way of representing those four types. We hope you'll agree.

Please remember that anyone can have more than one type of personality. You might already know someone who is a tough businessman at work, then spends his spare time doing charity work. You may know someone who is charming and generous when dealing with clients, but negotiates fiercely with suppliers. Or someone who keeps her head down at work, focusing on spreadsheets, then goes wild every Friday night. Anyone's personality can change on different days and in different situations. But you only need to focus on how they are when they are dealing with you, then tailor your approach to fit that type of personality.

As this is a book about business, and you are probably most bothered about making a good impression on your prospective customers, you'll see an emphasis on how to tailor your sales pitch to suit the different types of personality. This isn't rocket science, though – once you've understood the concept, you will be able to work out how to make a good impression in any other type of situation.

We spent a lot of time together on this, brainstorming (and mind mapping) our own definitions, to cover all the character types we have ever come across and the ways that we have found most successful in approaching those people. Now back to our eureka moment around representing the four different types of personality, which happens to be something we see every single day: THE SUITS ON PLAYING CARDS. They represent the four types more directly than any other system we've seen. For example, with colours – is yellow outgoing or caring? But there's no doubt that the heart represents someone who is loving and caring.

You will probably easily recognise yourself in one of these descriptions:

DIAMOND

Diamond characters are natural leaders, can be highly competitive and aren't afraid of taking risks. They can be charming, though that is usually only in order to gain control of a situation. To win over a diamond, remember that they value their time and can't bear it when other people don't stick to the point or to business. Try to control them or a situation, and you'll have lost them.

PERSONALITY
ALPHA (FE)MALE, NATURAL LEADER, GOAL-ORIENTATED, MONEY-FOCUSED, COMPETITIVE, LIKES CHALLENGE AND SOLVING PROBLEMS

WEAKNESSES
INSENSITIVE, INATTENTIVE TO DETAIL, IMPATIENT, OVERLOOKS RISKS

PITCH
FOCUS ON FINANCIAL OUTCOME AND PROFIT TO THEIR OWN AND THEIR BUSINESS DEVELOPMENT

——— DIAMOND ———

PERSONALITY
ORGANISED, DISCIPLINED, THOROUGH,
CALM, INDEPENDENT, ANALYTICAL

WEAKNESSES
INDECISIVE, HESITANT, SENSITIVE,
CAN GET BOGGED DOWN IN DETAIL

PITCH
DETAILED, FACTS-BASED BENEFITS OF
PRODUCT, PLUS CLEAR DETAILS OF HOW
IT WILL POSITIVELY IMPACT THE PERSON
AND/OR COMPANY OBJECTIVES

—— SPADE ——

SPADE

Spade characters are analytical, logical and conscientious. They'll need to know every detail of a situation before they'll sign on the dotted line. If anyone's going to check the terms and conditions, it will be the spade. They are often perfectionists and are happiest with a high-quality proposal that carries a guarantee. Get your facts lined up and don't turn up late, and you'll have made a good start with a spade.

HEART

Heart characters are generally relaxed, patient and easy to get along with. They can sometimes appear emotionally driven, reacting especially if someone seems insincere or insensitive. It's best to build trust with a heart character and not to dominate a conversation – they're easy to please, but they expect similar levels of respect in return.

PERSONALITY
GENEROUS, EAGER TO PLEASE, OPTIMISTIC,
HARD-WORKING, CHARITABLE

WEAKNESSES
SOMETIMES SELF-DOUBTING, SENSITIVE,
UNAMBITIOUS IN OWN GOALS

PITCH
LOW CHALLENGE – WILLING TO AGREE WITH
OTHERS AND ACCEPT ARGUMENTS – MAINLY
WANTING TO ENSURE THAT THE OUTCOME WILL
WORK WELL AND PLEASE EVERYONE

—— HEART ——

PERSONALITY
OUTGOING, CONFIDENT, EGOCENTRIC, PERSONALLY SUCCESSFUL, OPTIMISTIC, VERBALLY ARTICULATE, CREATES AN ENTERTAINING CLIMATE

WEAKNESSES
IMPULSIVE, NON-COMMITTAL, OVERAMBITIOUS, OVERESTIMATES RESULTS

PITCH
HIGH CHALLENGE - HARD TO PERSUADE - BEST TO LET THEM THINK SOMETHING WAS THEIR IDEA

CLUB

CLUB

Club characters are usually the life and soul of the party. They can be loud and vocal, but also friendly, loyal and family-orientated. They often fear rejection more than the other suits, and are great team players with just about any group. If you want to get a club on side, don't get too heavy with detail – they would rather have fun with people than focus only on business and tasks.

Again, you might find your personality crossing over into a different suit, especially in a particular situation. Think of someone you know well, and it will be just as easy to determine one or more suits for their personality. But how can you categorise someone you don't know well? It's probably much easier than you think.

You can get an immediate impression of someone's strongest suit as soon as you meet them, especially if their personality reminds you of someone else you know. You can also listen out for key words and preferences. If they're more interested in your life story than the product, you'll have met with a HEART. If they want to meet over lunch then chat about their weekend, you've probably found a CLUB. And if they focus on financial goals or details, you've most likely met a DIAMOND or a SPADE.

As soon as you have a pretty good idea of the suit you're dealing with, you can tailor your approach and communication to achieve the best results with that person. Flatter a HEART and focus on how your solution will please their boss and improve company results. Keep the conversation light with a CLUB; let them tell you about their weekend and take the credit for finding you. With a DIAMOND, don't try to lead the conversation, and keep a snappy emphasis on financial outcomes. Stick to the facts and praise a SPADE for their emphasis on detail, and you'll have made a valuable new connection.

Take time to try this out with family and friends, to realise just how powerful the results are when you focus on what's most important to the characteristics of any particular suit. Your more deliberate approach will help you make your partner feel less stressed about their day at work. You'll be able to create a more harmonious atmosphere at a family get-together. You'll be able to improve an existing friendship, by focusing on what's most important to the other person. And you will then be surprised how quickly you can get into the habit of applying the same approach and achieving improved results in business. For example, if you have a strained relationship with an existing client, you'll find ways to improve communication and make your own business more important to them. We have included specific 'pitch' tips next to each of the suit descriptions above, because this system can be especially effective in a sales situation. Whether you're trying to get your partner to agree with your plans for the weekend, or pitching your product or service to a global CEO, working out first what's most important to the other person will significantly improve your chances of a successful outcome.

BUILDING RAPPORT WITH OTHER PEOPLE

When it comes to building rapport, we are both lucky in that it comes pretty naturally to us. We don't feel uncomfortable about approaching strangers and we find it easy to establish fruitful relationships. However, in the same way that we think everyone should continually strive to improve their business and maintain growth, we never stop looking for ways to improve rapport with other people, especially the ways that don't necessarily come naturally to anyone. That has helped us not only to build stronger relationships, but to hone our skills at presenting and delivering training. We hope this section will help you to improve your rapport-building skills in three key areas.

Building trust to strengthen relationships. As we've said before, the strongest relationships and best sales results come when you share the same values and beliefs as your prospect, enabling them to trust you. It might be that you are entering a meeting with someone you have never spoken to, or have only exchanged emails with their PA, so you've had no means to establish what is most important to the decision maker. Don't panic – finding out about someone's values and beliefs is simply a matter of asking questions and listening. Ask a few questions, and you will be able to tell from their answers what is most important to them. Here's a list of the types of questions you can ask:

What is most important to you about . . . ?

What are your main goals this year?

What are your standard buying criteria?

What might cause you to change suppliers?

How soon would you like to achieve results in this area?

Is there anything about the service/product you use now that has been un/satisfactory?

Would you rather cut costs or increase productivity?

What level of service do you normally prefer?

How is your business doing at the moment?

What are your long-term business goals?

Answers to any of those questions will give you crucial information about what is most important to the other person or company, for example ROI, goals, urgency, quality, flexibility or cost. You can then tailor your approach, focusing on the type of solution that will deliver the most value to them. You won't be making anything up, just knowing how best to emphasise the benefits and solutions of what you are offering.

We have focused here on a sales-pitch situation, but you can apply exactly the same principles to any situation where you are engaging with another person and want to build a stronger relationship.

Some reassurance if you feel that you sometimes lack charisma.
You don't need to be ENTERTAINING or HILARIOUS for people to trust and like you. Remember these key points, and you will have other ways to create and strengthen your connections:

1. **Show interest in the other person.** Remember to ask them questions and listen with interest, rather than only telling them about what you do. It can help to show empathy by using a personal example of your own experience, but give the other person time to talk first and ask them further questions, before jumping in to tell them about you. Everyone LOVES to be listened to.

2. **Give genuine compliments.** Look out for things that you genuinely like about them. That could be their office, their website, something they have achieved – anything. Give genuine reasons for your admiration, and they will feel appreciated. In case we haven't mentioned the key word here enough times: be *genuine*. Nearly anyone can tell if you're not being 100% sincere, and that will have the opposite effect, diminishing their trust in you.

3. **Be relaxed and friendly.** If you know you'll feel nervous at tomorrow's meeting, practise today walking into the room and engaging in personal conversation before launching into business talk. The more relaxed you are, the easier others will find it to trust you. If your speech speeds up when you're nervous, make time to practise talking more slowly and deliberately, which in itself will make you seem more confident and increase other people's trust in you.

4. **Be appropriately light-hearted.** If you talk too earnestly about your product, or raise your voice when presenting the points you find important, the listener is much less likely to open up to what you are saying. You don't want to be informal with a key decision maker, but if they can relate to you on a personal level, they will be more likely to engage with you on a business level.

5. **Mirror body language, expressions, breathing and speech.** This takes a little practice – you don't want to make it even slightly obvious that you are copying someone else. Start with friends, and very subtly in business meetings. If the person you're talking to is standing with their arms crossed, after a while, fold your arms in front of you. If they are leaning back in their chair, make your stance more relaxed. Subtly mirror breathing, inhaling and exhaling in sync with the other person – they'll never notice, but the subliminal effect can be incredibly strong. Listen out for key words the other person uses and subtly drop them into your own speech. Talk at approximately the same speed, using similar patterns of pauses as the other person. If all this is sounding less than scientific, Google 'NLP mirroring' and you'll find all the information you need in order to understand and/or believe this process fully. Otherwise, just keep practising mirroring and you will start to notice how helpful it is in developing and building rapport.

Finally, some tips on how to work a crowd. This is clearly an area that's important to us, as speakers, trainers and entertainers. Even if you don't normally have to engage with a crowd, there will almost certainly be times when you meet with a a number of people from a company. It will be extremely beneficial for you to identify the most significant people to talk to and to know how to make the most impact on the whole group.

The most significant person – the strongest influencer – won't always be the person of highest seniority in the company. We're not sure we need to tell you how to identify the alpha character in a group – you will normally know within minutes, just by watching how everyone is interacting. The alpha will be the person everyone else stops to listen to. He'll be entertaining, with everyone hanging on his every word. He can laugh at himself, but other people will almost certainly laugh warmheartedly then turn the joke around onto someone else. In short, he's the strongest presence in the room, and it won't take long for you to identify him.

Hey – we're not being sexist here – we just don't want to keep writing 'he or she'. In our experience, though, if there are males and females in a room, nine times out of ten the alpha is male.

AS SOON AS YOU HAVE IDENTIFIED THE ALPHA AND WON HIM OVER, JUST ABOUT EVERYONE ELSE IN THE ROOM WILL BE ON SIDE. But that can be easier said than done – the alpha will be a strong leader (probably a diamond) who is hard to please. He won't be afraid of challenging you and isn't going to have sympathy if he sees you struggling. Spencer remembers his learning process from early in his career:

'There was this gig, early on in my journey. I was a young guy, single at the time, so not the easiest person for other guys to have entertaining them and their partners. I went up to the first group and offered to show them some magic. The first guy turned to me, looked me straight in the eyes and point blank told me to leave. His girlfriend then turned to him and said, "No, I want to see this", which made the situation even worse. He got up and walked off to the bar, at which point his mates agreed with him and walked off as well. So now – the last thing they would have wanted – I'm left doing magic with just their partners. I'm effectively moving in on their girlfriends . . . and straight into fight territory.

'If I ever performed first to a group of women, by the time I went over to the guys, they now "owned" me. "Oh, so you've finally worked up the courage to come and see us, have you? Now that you've had enough fun with our birds?" It wouldn't matter then if I was the best magician in the world – any chance of support would be gone – they'd put me down to everyone else there for the rest of the night.

'So I turned it around. I started approaching a group of guys first, to interact with them and get them on side. They'd usually start off by trying to find ways to catch me out. I wouldn't try and take control – I'd say, "Of course you'll catch me out – you're superior to me!". There'd be no better feeling than when I'd completed the first round of magic and the guys were on side. They'd tell everyone else about me, praising me for the rest of the night … and then they'd OFFER their partners to me, "Oh, you've got to see this fella here, I'm going to leave you with him". No conflict – everyone's happy.'

Spencer's examples here are from a specific type of environment, but you get the picture. It's also important to remember that you won't always be able to win over a crowd or even a small group of people. There will always be someone who just doesn't value what you do or like how you talk to them. There will always be some chance of conflict in any type of situation. As your confidence builds, thanks to the progress you have made in winning other people over, you will learn not to take the knocks personally, instead simply accepting less successful meetings as part of your own learning experience.

LOOK BACK AND HELP SOMEONE ELSE UP

If you skipped the introduction, or if you can't remember the content, please go back and look now at the benefits we have found in helping other people to become more successful.

In short:

COLLABORATION
Mutual reward from helping others

CONTENTMENT
The feel-good factor in seeing someone you've helped succeed

CONSEQUENCES
The all-round benefits from other companies and the economy flourishing

NATALIE WINTER, DIRECTOR AT QUBE RECRUITMENT, is a good friend of Spencer's and a true ambassador for this section. Natalie's primary focus is her son – she wants to inspire him to work hard, while always keeping his feet on the ground. Her second priority and overriding source of satisfaction is helping other people to do well: 'Success in my head is where we are now. We've turned Qube Recruitment around 150% in the last year, and we've done it as a team. We've supported each other. For me, success is seeing other people succeed. My PA, Sarah, started as a receptionist, as meek as they come. Now she's my right arm – I couldn't do this without her. I'm having all the ideas, and she gets it and organises it. She also reins me in! That for me is success – people treating other people well, earning well from it, and enjoying it. We have to support each other – we're a work family, and it's amazing to witness the difference in people. We've still got lots to learn. But if you can enjoy what you do every day, you're very lucky. The buzz of ringing someone up and telling them you've got them a job is incredible. Delivering that kind of news to people – what could be better? I'm also passionate about the charity stuff we do – that's a really good feeling.

We're working now with a company that improves literacy. It costs us to do that, but we've made the money and can afford to support it. We meet so many youngsters who don't have the confidence to look you in the eye. I don't care what's on your CV – I was a nightmare at school, but it doesn't mean I'm any better or worse than you. It's about empowering people who come through our door – putting the best of them on their CV. We've met so many clients who ask for A–C grades, but wouldn't you prefer to work with someone who can hold a conversation, that you have a connection with? Sarah took the time recently to persuade a client about someone – he had bad grades, but Sarah said, 'TRUST ME'. They did, and they love him. Seeing someone come out of their shell and flourish is amazing. Money doesn't give you a cuddle at night. I take my son away, and I currently have to save to do that, but then I know I've achieved it. If you can just buy what you want, surely it comes to the point where it doesn't mean anything. How you treat me will mean more to me than what you've ever got monetary-wise.'

While researching for this book, a number of people have given their time and made the effort to meet up with us. The most important point to note here is that it has been a two-way process. We have given them free advice on how to improve their businesses, and they have helped us to target and develop specific areas for the book. Some of those people have made significant progress thanks to the advice they took on board, and their feedback since the meetings has given us powerful personal motivation and extra belief in what we are delivering. We've also made long-lasting connections with likeminded entrepreneurs, who are keen to learn more and will no doubt keep on promoting what we do. They're not taking business from either of us, and it's almost certain we will have picked up tips from them, on things they do differently. And you almost can't beat the feeling when you hear back from them, finding out you've helped someone to improve their life, enjoy their business more and feel happier. All this from a few relaxing hours of animated conversation, chatting over coffee and lunch at Hermitage Road, a fantastic restaurant and bar in Hitchin. A massive win-win situation.

THERE'S NO RUSH OR PRESSURE TO START HELPING OTHER PEOPLE UP. It clearly isn't going to be a priority or even very fruitful when you are first starting out. While you're still creating all your own processes and goals, it's unlikely you'll be able to give much practical advice to other people. But please make a resolute and positive decision now, that when you are at the right stage in your business, you will be happy to share advice and help other people to get to where you are. It doesn't even need to cost you anything, apart from the time it takes to speak to or meet up with people. And we promise that you will gain from the relationship in a number of ways, potentially even more than the person you're helping.

We've given you two perspectives so far on helping other people up. Natalie Winter, who is incredibly successful in business, despite (or thanks to?) her selfless determination to help other people. Then a slightly more selfish view from us, enjoying helping others but also valuing the advantages that we gain from doing it. We'll finish this chapter with some feedback from Paul Fowler, an excellent magician and entertainer who has achieved fantastic growth since starting up on his own. Spencer acted as Paul's mentor when he was starting out, then we both gave him some work and encouragement later on. We didn't feed him lines, by the way – this all comes directly from Paul, in an interview with our copy-editor.

PAUL FOWLER, FELLOW MAGICIAN AND CORPORATE INFOTAINER

I first met Spencer in 2010, when I was still in a full-time job. I was in a magic club and knew I wanted to set up my own business one day, but at that point had no experience of the business side of magic. I live near Spencer and had heard his name mentioned a few times, as someone who was very successful in the industry. Then, one night I was at a club, Spencer was there. I didn't know who he was at first, but there was this very confident presence in the room and I decided to go and have a chat with him. I was very nervous, but I showed him a couple of tricks, and he gave me some positive feedback.

We linked up on Facebook, and started having calls now and again. Spencer asked how I was doing and how I was going to grow my business, but I didn't have any plan at that point. He very kindly offered to give me some tips and ideas, and I started going along and helping Spencer at his gigs. I walked around filming on an iPad, which took the pressure off me while I watched how he operated in a room full of corporate clients. He also taught me how to do wedding fairs, and before long started passing on any double-booked dates he had.

It really was a luxury type of relationship for me, which I could never have anticipated. Spencer kept giving me jobs he couldn't cover and tested me with harder jobs, to see if I could handle the pressure. I've always been the type of person to say yes to any job, but the confidence to take the leap of faith really came from Spencer's support. I didn't really know anyone else in the industry well enough to ask questions, but I could just call Spencer up whenever I had a question about the business side of things.

Having a full-time job first did benefit me. If anyone asked for my advice as they were leaving school, I would probably tell them to go and get a job with other people first, to learn how to interact with people in the outside world. That's something you need to be able to do to succeed in your own business. I'd started off as an engineer when I left school and I learnt very quickly how to work in a trade-type of environment, how to interact with that kind of person. Then I went into business development and sales because I wanted to learn how to interact on a corporate level and how to sell my own business.

Really, up to going full-time, all the pieces were put into place for me; I just needed to make that jump. I think that everyone in life can create that opportunity. They just have to know, when the opportunity comes, that they have to go for it. A lot of people compare their situation with yours – they ask you about what you're doing, and they're looking for pieces of information that don't tie in with their life, to give them a reason for why they can't do the same. Everyone's situation is unique, but you've got to make that work for you. You've just got to say yes to situations. Even if it means learning a new skill – you can learn that on the way to doing the job – just put yourself out of your comfort zone.

I had been daydreaming for years about giving up my day job in business development. Then, in 2014, I got the impression that my boss wasn't going to keep me on after the Christmas period, which rang some alarm bells in my head. I realised that I could either go and get another sales job, and potentially have the same thing happen three months later, or I could try doing something for myself and see how it went. I wrote myself a business plan. I had very little money – basically eight months before I would have to go and get another job. But I'm pleased to say that after two or three months, I had tripled my planned revenue. It is the best thing I have ever done.

My whole first year of being a full-time magician, I would speak to Spencer every day, as I pretty much still do. The next year, he introduced me to Lee, who was very well recognised in the industry. I told Lee a bit of my story, which I think he respected, then I got a call from him, offering me a gig he couldn't cover. Lee also gave me an introduction to trade shows. He showed me what to look out for on the stands – ones that should have had a high footfall but didn't. Then Spencer said, 'Why don't you go and offer 30 minutes for free on that stand and show them exactly what you can do for them?' It was a bold thing to do, but I did it. I didn't get anything directly from that, but then I did exactly the same at another trade show sometime later, which has led to a client booking me for five trade shows – they just keep coming back to book me again.

It was lifechanging, having the tips from Spencer and Lee on putting myself out there. Then having that support from them, watching what they did and how relaxed they were while they were doing it. They said to me: 'You want it. There it is – just go and get it.'

I'm really satisfied with where I am now – my growth has been very rapid. That's down to the mentoring I had from Lee and Spencer, but also due to the passion I have for not going back to what I did for 14 years before this. The other driving force is wanting to support myself, my fiancée, and my family in the future, as well as affording some luxuries, and to be able to get those off my own back, not relying on someone else to do it for me. I was always jumping from job to job after I left school, and I was never happy working for someone else – something I only fully realised when I became self-employed! It was only when I met Spencer and got more into magic that it gave me direction and belief in what I wanted to do.

Reading as well is another huge part. It can be lonely, working on your own, and it's encouraging knowing that other people are going through the same things as you. The books I've read have created revenue for me, and they helped to motivate me and change my mindset. Sometimes I really had to dig deep, to take on a contract out of my comfort zone. But anything that's very difficult for me, I treat as a project, so I dedicate time out of my diary for those projects, which makes them go very well. I'll physically have put in the time and the effort, to make sure that the client gets what they have asked for.

There was something I heard ages ago, that has stayed in my mind and made a real difference to me: 'There's no such thing as a mistake if you make it once'. There are times when I've made mistakes, then I haven't beaten myself up about it. If I make the same mistake two or three times, I might be being incompetent. But any mistake I make just once is part of a learning process.

I don't feel ready to be a mentor yet, but I am sure I will do it one day. Right now, I'm just trying to get to my own top level, but then I am always giving people advice when I can. I also pass on work to the semi-professional magicians who are now where I was a few years ago, to try and help them on their journey. Some people say it helps to talk to someone who's relatively new in the business, and my journey is still very fresh. The book The Go-Giver tells you that if you give something back to people, all of a sudden, new opportunities create themselves. That's what I've learnt from Spencer as well – he is extremely good at relationship-building and he'll help people out, then all of a sudden that comes full circle and an opportunity arises for him.

I've now started to go off in my own direction, mainly due to the confidence I've gained over the last few years working with Spencer and Lee. We all still talk and get together and know what's going on in each other's lives. I'm getting married soon and Spencer's going to be my best man. And yes, we are going to have a magician on our wedding day!

CHAPTER 11
Raise the stakes

The fact that you are reading Chapter 11 shows that you have a respectable level of dedication. Some people will have given up halfway through, while others – like a couple of people we have met on our journey – will have resisted change and stuck to their own ways of doing everything.

Well done for sticking with us – give yourself a pat on the back, especially if you've already taken some of our advice on board. As we've said before, you have to remember to feel good about anything and everything you achieve, and even just making the effort to read the whole book demonstrates your commitment to finding ways to develop your business.

NOW WE'RE RAISING THE STAKES

This final chapter might only be for the most committed, the people who will always be willing to keep striving hard to achieve more in life and in business. Don't take any discouragement from that – this is a feel-good chapter, to help motivate anyone who has the desire to keep achieving higher potential. There is no way that you need to have been the highest achiever at school, in your day job or in running your own business, in order to aim for the top. **Regardless of where you are now, as long as you have found something that you enjoy and can make money from, you only need to take specific actions in sufficient quantities in order to reach higher levels of success.** As long as you keep aiming higher, there will be no limit to your potential.

Think of this final chapter as your three power tools. Keep coming back to it, to remind yourself of what you need to do in order to keep aiming higher, no matter what stage you have reached. We'll start with two ways to help you to reach new goals. Then we'll come back to our Buddy Up System, to give you encouragement and advice on why and how you can benefit from finding a likeminded partner in business.

TICK ALL THE BOXES

In the introduction we said that, even if you acted on only one piece of advice and saw improvements to your business, we would be satisfied that the book had been a success.

FORGET THAT. WE NOW WANT YOU TO FOLLOW *ALL* THE STEPS.

The structure of this book originated, of course, from a mind map. Like any of our mind maps, it's a work in progress. We might add or change parts in subsequent editions of the book or for different seminars, talks and training courses, but on the next pages you'll find the mind map as it was when this book went to print. The page after that shows the same information in a checklist.

It's up to you how you use this – you can transfer the mind map to an app or a massive wall chart in your home or office. You could photocopy the checklist or write in your book. Or it will take minutes to create your own customised checklist, leaving out areas that aren't applicable to your line of business or adding others that are. **But don't leave any point out just because it's out of your comfort zone.**

Look back at any or all of the sections in this book, to refresh your memory about anything you're not sure of – the points on the mind map and the checklist come in the same order as the chapters and subsections, so they'll be easy to find in the book.

Keep the list in your mind and to hand, as a constant reminder of everything you need to focus on. If, ultimately, you apply yourself to every single area we have recommended, we are 100% confident you will see phenomenal changes to your business and personal life. It might take you a few months to adopt all the steps, but it is a simple process of working through a list and feeling good every time you can add a tick next to anything you have taken on board and/or mastered.

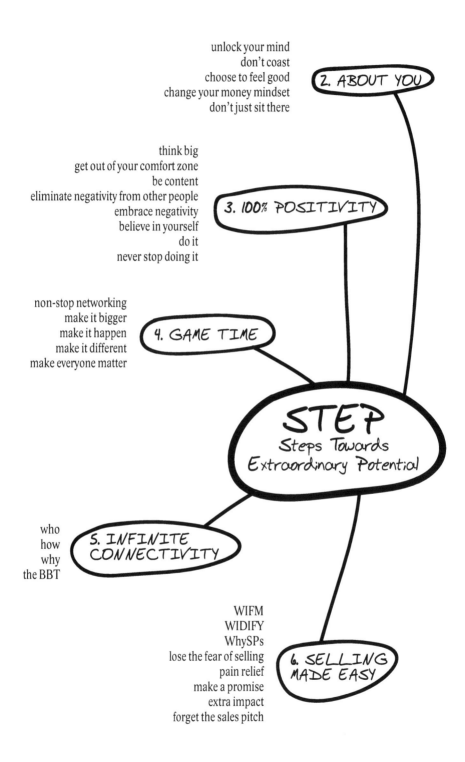

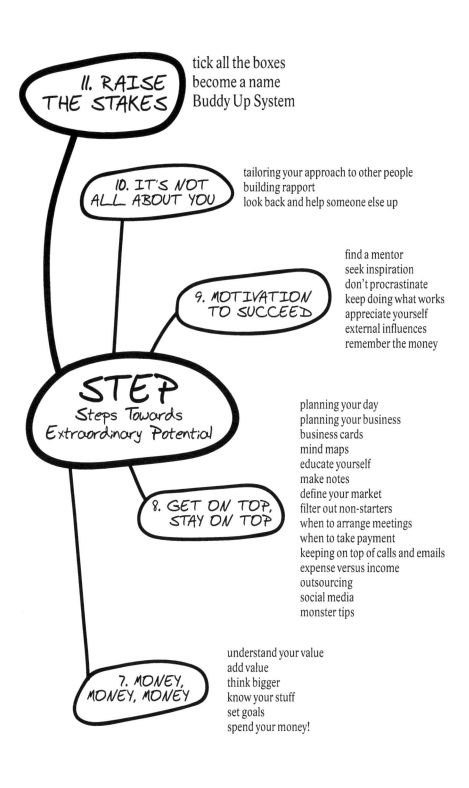

11. RAISE THE STAKES
tick all the boxes
become a name
Buddy Up System

10. IT'S NOT ALL ABOUT YOU
tailoring your approach to other people
building rapport
look back and help someone else up

9. MOTIVATION TO SUCCEED
find a mentor
seek inspiration
don't procrastinate
keep doing what works
appreciate yourself
external influences
remember the money

STEP
Steps Towards
Extraordinary Potential

8. GET ON TOP, STAY ON TOP
planning your day
planning your business
business cards
mind maps
educate yourself
make notes
define your market
filter out non-starters
when to arrange meetings
when to take payment
keeping on top of calls and emails
expense versus income
outsourcing
social media
monster tips

7. MONEY, MONEY, MONEY
understand your value
add value
think bigger
know your stuff
set goals
spend your money!

STEP CHECKLIST

2. ABOUT YOU
- ☐ unlock your mind
- ☐ don't coast
- ☐ choose to feel good
- ☐ change your money mindset
- ☐ don't just sit there

3. 100% POSITIVITY
- ☐ think big
- ☐ get out of your comfort zone
- ☐ be content
- ☐ eliminate negativity from other people
- ☐ embrace negativity
- ☐ believe in yourself
- ☐ do it
- ☐ never stop doing it

4. GAME TIME
- ☐ non-stop networking
- ☐ make it bigger
- ☐ make it happen
- ☐ make it different
- ☐ make everyone matter

5. INFINITE CONNECTIVITY
- ☐ who
- ☐ how
- ☐ why
- ☐ the BBT

6. SELLING MADE EASY
- ☐ WIFM
- ☐ WIDIFY
- ☐ WhySPs
- ☐ lose the fear of selling
- ☐ pain relief
- ☐ make a promise
- ☐ extra impact
- ☐ forget the sales pitch

7. MONEY, MONEY, MONEY
- ☐ understand your value
- ☐ add value
- ☐ think bigger
- ☐ know your stuff
- ☐ set goals
- ☐ spend your money!

8. GET ON TOP, STAY ON TOP
- ☐ planning your day
- ☐ planning your business
- ☐ business cards
- ☐ mind maps
- ☐ educate yourself
- ☐ make notes
- ☐ define your market
- ☐ filter out non-starters
- ☐ when to arrange meetings
- ☐ when to take payment
- ☐ keeping on top of calls and emails
- ☐ expense versus income
- ☐ outsourcing
- ☐ social media
- ☐ monster tips

9. MOTIVATION TO SUCCEED
- ☐ find a mentor
- ☐ seek inspiration
- ☐ don't procrastinate
- ☐ keep doing what works
- ☐ appreciate yourself
- ☐ external influences
- ☐ remember the money

10. IT'S NOT ALL ABOUT YOU
- ☐ tailoring your approach to other people
- ☐ building rapport
- ☐ look back and help someone else up

11. RAISE THE STAKES
- ☐ tick all the boxes
- ☐ become a name
- ☐ Buddy Up System

If you're right now looking at that list and wondering how you'll be able to cover all the points, start by working again on the points about mindset that we raised in Chapters 2 and 3. You might even only need to review the subheadings, as they're listed on the mind map and checklist on the previous pages. It was actually hard for us to start this book talking about mindset and positivity, when we had so many practical tools lined up, but here's the critical statement that we 100% stand by: **Mindset is a game changer – it's the difference between success and failure.** Every single point is easily achievable – it's the sum total of all of them that will give you exceptional results.

STEPS TOWARDS *EXTRAORDINARY* POTENTIAL.

We're not going to have time to respond to feedback and queries from everyone who reads this. But when you have taken all the steps we have recommended (including the ones in this chapter), please feel free to contact us to give constructive feedback, ask about anything that isn't working for you, or to tell us about how you are getting on.

BECOME A NAME

Modesty aside – we both often have people say to us 'Know what? I've seen a lot of magicians in my time, but you're in a different class', or something very similar. And yet we honestly don't consider ourselves to be the best magicians in the country. We manipulate decks of cards and perform tricks very similarly to other magicians. But we add value to our act and our service, and constantly strive to improve our business processes, to make sure we're different from everyone else. And we have become names in our industry.

In all our meetings while we were researching for the book, the word 'dominate' kept cropping up, but that can too easily be misconstrued. Each of us wants to become the best in our field, in specific geographical markets and specific business areas. We are ambitious enough to want to become the highest earners and most prominent figures in particular markets, so when we started off discussing all this, we talked about how we wanted to dominate in those areas. But we realised the word 'dominate' could imply negative levels of control and competition. We don't have any aspirations to outshine our peers at their expense. Hey, we would hardly be writing this book if that were the case.

We do want to inspire other business owners to keep striving to become a name in any area in which they love working. Each of us can already safely claim to be the first person that anyone – in our industry and in our geographical areas – thinks of when anyone talks about wedding magicians. Lee has become THE wedding magician in Hertfordshire; Spencer has become THE wedding magician in Kent. And those geographical areas keep stretching – there's a good number of people in surrounding counties, including London, that will think of us first whenever they hear of someone who needs a magician for a wedding.

We don't yet get the same level of recognition in the trade show market, for example, or in other areas such as speaking and business-development training. But we're working hard at changing that by increasing our activity in a multitude of different areas, using all the tools in this book.

You'll notice the emphasis here on collaboration. We're not competing with each other. We're not competing with other magicians or putting anyone else down in order to raise our own profiles or dominate the market. There's a phenomenal amount of power in genuine motivation, and all of the most highly motivated people we know accept that working together with other people is essential to their success. The more we team up with other people, the closer we get to being top of our game, and to becoming a name in a particular area of our business.

To become 'the ...' in your field, you have to keep striving to be brilliant. You have to persist until you are well established. You have to deliver a consistently high-quality product, service and image of yourself, until the top clients in any market want to book you or buy from you. Then you will become a name – the person that other people look up to – and teaming up with likeminded peers will get you there even faster.

If you put in, you get back – it's as simple as that. If you generally push yourself hard enough, take enough action AND help other people, you get rewarded for it. Even in bad situations, if you stay positive, you'll grow and stay strong. As soon as you understand these principles, it will be easier to stay focused on the end goal of getting to the top and becoming a name in your line of business.

BUDDY UP SYSTEM

To us, our Buddy Up System is the epitome of collaboration. We are still amazed by the difference it has made to both of our businesses as well as its ongoing positive impact. Both our wives regularly remind us never to fall out with each other, because of the enormous financial benefits of our partnership.

Our Buddy Up System is a ridiculously easy concept to understand. It has countless advantages, with minimal restrictions or drawbacks. What amazes us most is that we haven't found anyone else doing it. Apart from the people we know, that is. There are some peer-network models, where similar businesses share ideas or cooperate on a specific contract. There are industry-specific forums and some support networks. It's pretty standard for companies to partner up with others, to fulfil one project or provide a multifaceted service. But we have yet to find any business advice that recommends anything similar to our system.

You'll find out about the origins of our Buddy Up System at the end of this chapter, in the interview with Richard Redding. Before that, we're going to round off our part of this final chapter by showing you how to establish your own successful Buddy Up relationship. It's the longest section yet, but that doesn't make it difficult – these are straightforward steps, advice and tips on how to maximise your potential.

1. THE ESSENTIALS

This isn't just about collaboration. It's not only about sharing business ideas or working together on projects. And it isn't about forming a network group or helping another person with their business.

This is about finding the right business partner and establishing a rock-solid system, based on the advice in the rest of this chapter. Within a very short time, you will both be able to experience mindblowing improvements to your businesses, WITH MASSIVE VALUE AND RETURNS.

Our Buddy Up System is the opposite of competition. It's about TWO PEOPLE NOT COMPETING WITH EACH OTHER, BUT COMBINING FORCES in ways that more than double any individual effort.

It is vital that you don't look at a potential buddy wondering what they can do for you. From this point forward, you will need to FOCUS ON WHAT YOU CAN ACHIEVE TOGETHER, TO DELIVER BETTER RESULTS FOR BOTH OF YOU. You will then be working together to make more money for the whole partnership, and to make your team more dynamic and effective.

As soon as you have found the right business partner and established your own Buddy Up System, you will find that there is NO COMPETITION between you. It's around this time that you will probably start talking as 'we', which we'll explain more in point 3, THE WAY FORWARD.

With a Buddy Up System, YOU CAN ONLY INCREASE YOUR INCOME – YOU CAN'T DAMAGE IT. People who don't get that don't fully understand the power of networking and, in our opinion, aren't going to do well in business.

Before we started this, we were each other's direct competitors. Now that we are a team, we have removed the competition – right now, our competition can't touch us. How much fun is that, to think that two guys who were competing are now dominating?

2. THE GROUNDWORK

FINDING A BUDDY

You clearly can't partner up with just anyone, and this isn't something you should rush into. Until you find your ideal Buddy Up partner, simply work hard at all the other areas of this book. Your increased success levels will give you confidence and experience, as well as connecting you with a higher number of potential business partners. Then keep the following points in mind, and you will one day find your ideal buddy.

Someone you already know?

The longer you've been in business, the more likely it will be that you already know at least one person you could consider as your Buddy Up partner. Take time to think about who – in your circle of peers and associates – you could trust and work with. Even if someone seems right, if you feel you can't trust them, you *must* find someone else. If they can't share work unconditionally, you don't want to be in with that person.

Similar ethos

After trust, this is the most important component to a strong Buddy Up relationship. By 'ethos' we mean that you both have to have similar attitudes, aims, drive, energy and enthusiasm. You've got to find someone who is as hungry as you, as busy as you, and willing to put as much effort in as you. Note the word 'similar', though – there will always be some differences. You will learn from and feed off each other, but it might be impossible to have a really successful relationship if you both have completely different essential priorities and levels of drive.

Different abilities

We'll explain more about identifying and benefiting from your different strengths and weaknesses later in this chapter. For now, while you are working at finding your ideal buddy, you need to remember that the strongest Buddy Up System will come from two people who bring different skills, qualifications and talents to the table. If your buddy is too similar to you, you won't benefit from the ideal combination of expertise.

The competition?

If you were to partner up with someone who is much more, or much less, established and experienced than you, it would become more of a mentoring than a Buddy Up relationship. Whatever the stage of your business, it could be best to look at your direct competition. It might take some time to break down potential barriers – it's likely your closest competitor wouldn't immediately see the benefit of partnering up with you. And it might be that they never do – if you've been trying too hard or too long to connect with them, it's very likely they won't have the right mentality for a Buddy Up relationship in the first place. Leave them behind and look for someone else.

Further afield

If there are no ideal partners close to where you are based, look around on Facebook etc to find people further afield. It might be more hassle to arrange meetings, but on the plus side, you are both likely to expand your target business areas.

Corresponding businesses

We have so far found huge benefits from working closely with the people who are in the same lines of business as us, but we are now working at *complementary* Buddy Up Systems. Whatever your area of business, there will be people offering different things to the same types of clients. It might help you to partner up with someone who has the same level of creativity, similar technical experience, and/or matching client bases, even though your products or services are quite different. If you can't find a buddy in your own line of work, keep thinking outside the box until you find someone else with whom you could establish a mutually profitable partnership.

If you can't find a buddy . . .

Be patient. Keep working hard at your own business, while keeping all this in mind, and you will one day get there. Until then, go back to Chapter 10 and consider mentoring someone who's starting out. It's still a mutually beneficial activity, and before you know it, the person you're mentoring could be up to your level and have the perfect mentality to join you in a Buddy Up System.

COMMUNICATION!

Communication surely has to be the most important factor in any successful business or personal relationship. You probably already know that, but we HAVE to emphasise it here as being the vital component of the Buddy Up System. Here are four points that are vital to successful communication with your buddy.

Start off on the right foot

Right from the start, you need to communicate about how you are going to keep the lines of communication open. You need to make it clear that, if there is any ongoing breakdown in or disagreement about communication, it will be easier simply to part ways.

Raise (and respect) any concerns

You have to agree at the start that there will be differences in opinions. It would be almost weird if two people worked together and agreed on everything. You both have to feel comfortable, from the start, in raising concerns and not taking offence if the other person does. At the same time, you both have to be respectful and impersonal, keeping this firmly about business.

Agree on work processes

Between you, you'll already have experience of the work and challenges you'll face, such as volume of emails and difficult customers. It's ideal to present a united front, as a partnership, to make it clear that you work compatibly and professionally. We therefore highly recommend you work together to identify the types of scenarios you will face and agree in advance on things like response times, complaint handling and dealing with late payments. Over time, you can work at making factors such as marketing and email content compatible within the partnership. You're not aiming to be clones of each other, but unity and consistency will give your clients more respect for your partnership.

Maintain mutual trust and respect

This is largely self-explanatory, but you must remember that trust and respect are essential to a successful Buddy Up. Remember, too, that if either of you is guarding work, contacts or knowledge, you're not going to connect – it's back to being in competition.

NO CONTRACT

The very basis for the Buddy Up System is mutual reward through collaboration and trust. We suppose there will always be some circumstances, for example where large sums of money are involved, where you might feel the need to make a formal black-and-white agreement. We have never done that. And if you feel you need a contract for your whole partnership, you're not entering a genuine Buddy Up relationship.

NOT having a contract has the following benefits:

Positivity

The trust, bonhomie and enthusiasm of a friendship wins hands down against any business set-up.

Informality

Without a contract, you won't have concrete and measurable expectations from or towards your partner. The Buddy Up System is about having fun at being successful, not judging each other's performance.

Easy exit

This is the crux. You both need to communicate and agree from the start that, if anyone feels the relationship isn't working, you'll simply part ways. You don't need to worry – if you are pulling your weight and putting in enough effort, you will become indispensable to your buddy. As long as you don't have a contract, your buddy will be working hard to make you want to stay partnered up with them.

DISCUSS YOUR CORE BELIEFS AND AIMS

You will have already found a buddy with a similar ethos to yours. Now dig deeper. Arrange meetings, make time for phone calls and keep mind mapping to work out mutually agreeable aims that you can both work towards.

Your aims don't have to be identical, but you definitely need to be going in the same direction. And you have to settle on some core beliefs that are acceptable to you both. For example, is money the overriding priority? Do you both want to focus most on helping others? Are you both going to aim to hit a certain market or to work abroad?

IT IS VERY LIKELY THAT THIS STAGE OF THE PROCESS WILL GIVE YOU A SUDDEN UNDERSTANDING OF THE POTENTIAL OF THE BUDDY UP SYSTEM.

Formalising beliefs and considering new priorities can be surprisingly therapeutic. Accepting that you can work towards the new aims you uncovered in your mind mapping will open your eyes to levels of potential you would otherwise not even have considered.

We hope that you will at this point start to feel whole new levels of confidence in and commitment to your own business. We anticipate that you will come away from your first meetings feeling elated, energised and confident about what you can achieve. If you're feeling like that, don't allow any feelings of doubt to creep in. Instead, go back and read the epigraph at the start of this book, and allow yourself to believe that you can achieve anything.

3. THE WAY FORWARD

KEEP COMMUNICATING (ABOUT EVERYTHING)

Your Buddy Up relationship needs to keep evolving. It's no good deciding on some aims and sticking to them for ten years! The whole point of the Buddy Up System is to reach new levels of success and to keep challenging your levels of potential, so we urge you to keep talking and meeting up regularly to redefine your aims, challenge your levels of achievement and congratulate each other on the results you are achieving. Here are four essential tools to maximise the results from your communication.

Listen!

It's been said before: listening is the most important part of communication. However enthusiastic or certain you feel about an idea, please never forget that your partner's opinion is just as important (and you'll probably be surprised by how often they're right!). It is essential to keep encouraging ideas from both sides to make the most from any Buddy Up. One of you is bound to be less vocal or less sure of their ideas – if that person is overpowered, you'll be losing out on one half of the potential output of your partnership.

Set goals

Once you have agreed on the main aims, vision or mission of your partnership, it will be relatively easy to determine all the goals you need to achieve to get there. We've got to say this again – we have yet to find someone who hasn't been blown away by the power of mind mapping, and it makes goal setting incredibly easy. Even if it's something neither of you is currently keen on, please give it a go.

Identify strengths and weaknesses

This is the perfect example of the benefits of buddying up with someone who brings different skills to the table. For example, one of you might be better at prospecting and sales, while the other person excels at social media and marketing. Work out your different strengths and weaknesses so that you can each work on things you do best and enjoy most. Please remember this is subject to change – you'll learn from each other and likely discover hidden talents, so keep communicating about your strengths and weaknesses.

Allot tasks

When you have identified goals, decide who's going to do what, based on your strengths and weaknesses. You're probably already realising the potential here – for example, if you hate keeping track of payments and invoices, what a relief it will be if your buddy doesn't mind managing all that.

KEEP COMING BACK TO THIS CHAPTER

Even though you trust each other and work well together, challenges and stress are inevitable in any business situation. Don't even consider a Buddy Up with someone who hasn't read this book, or at least this chapter. And keep referring to it if or whenever you're experiencing doubts or challenges within your partnership.

BE FLEXIBLE, COMPATIBLE AND POSITIVE

As we've said before, it can be easiest to air worries or take any stress out on the person you work most closely with. You'll need to talk about concerns, but don't allow yourself to treat your buddy as your sounding board for all your worries.

Otherwise, remember that you don't have a contract. You need to make the effort to stay flexible and compatible, to maintain your value as a business partner, before your buddy finds someone else who's easier to work with.

MANAGE MONEY CAREFULLY

We are lucky enough to have a level of trust between us that doesn't require constant monitoring of finances. However, there is no doubt that money can be the biggest and easiest cause of dispute, even between close family members. While we strongly recommend against a contract for your whole Buddy Up relationship, it is essential that you both have 100% trust and awareness of any money you earn together or invest in your businesses.

We're not going to try to give specific advice on this – we're not financial experts or lawyers, and the level of control will depend on your own circumstances. Just please keep your eyes open and don't ever do anything that might endanger the trust that your buddy has for you. Lecture over. Apart from one other point:

Don't take money from your buddy
This is closely related to the 'Spend your money!' section in Chapter 7. You MUST get into the mindset of being generous, sharing and working towards a common goal. If you are worrying about having to pass on one big contract or a few jobs in one month, you have to keep in mind that you are working as a team, not in competition. If your partner consistently brings in lower-priced jobs or doesn't source new business, over an extended period, you will need to re-evaluate – the Buddy Up System is about equal partnership, not mentoring.

ALWAYS 'WE'
At least a year before we wrote this book or formalised our Buddy Up System, people would start asking who made up the 'we' either of us kept referring to. We hadn't even realised we were doing it. We'd informally started sharing work and discussing ideas, which soon led to multiple daily phone calls and close collaboration on any new initiative. And we were presenting ourselves as a united team to anyone with whom we discussed anything related to our businesses.

We didn't even say 'someone I work with' or 'my business partner and I'. We had simply established such a healthy level of trust and compatibility that we both kept using 'we' in any business situation. We know this might not last for ever – that's the nature of any Buddy Up – but right now, it's incredible to have established such a mutually rewarding partnership.

This isn't a requirement of the Buddy Up System, but you could recognise it as a positive sign if or when you find yourself comfortable with talking about you and your buddy as 'we'. When people pointed it out to us, we suddenly realised the level of trust and collaboration we'd been fortunate enough to reach.

Even if you never get comfortable with using 'we' when talking about your relationship with your buddy, please don't forget that there are huge advantages to presenting a united front. For example, if you say 'I can't do that date but I work with someone else who might be able to help', the client will probably think they're getting second best. But if you make it clear that you and your buddy share all bookings and present the same image, quality and service, the client will have the same level of trust and be grateful for your flexibility.

4. POTENTIAL ISSUES

When we first mapped out this Buddy Up System section, we brainstormed to think of potential issues people could face. We only came up with four headings, which are self-explanatory:

FINANCIAL DISCORD
IMBALANCE OF POWER/ENERGY/DEDICATION
HIDDEN AGENDAS
COMMUNICATION BREAKDOWN

Any of these could have a significantly negative effect on the success of any Buddy Up. And we genuinely believe that there are two straightforward solutions, which we have already covered in this chapter.

Constant and open communication will uncover and address the first three headings above: financial discord, imbalance of power/ energy/dedication, and hidden agendas.

If you are still having problems after that, it is likely that the fourth heading – communication breakdown – will be the root of any problems you're experiencing. Whether you can't talk openly to your buddy, or if they are reluctant to communicate regularly and/or honestly with you, we come back to the benefits we outlined earlier of having **no contract.** If communication isn't working properly or at all, you will need to accept that your Buddy Up relationship hasn't worked this time. We'll come back to our statement under point 2 in this section, THE GROUNDWORK: You both need to communicate and agree from the start that, if either of you feels the relationship isn't working, you'll simply part ways. If you have completed the groundwork, we hope you will find it easy to break free from your dysfunctional Buddy Up and that any negative fallout will be short-lived.

5. THE PERKS

SHARING TASKS, STRENGTHS AND WEAKNESSES

We won't repeat everything we said about this earlier in this chapter, but we have to remind you here of the huge benefits you'll get from sharing your skills and availability.

LEARNING FROM EACH OTHER

This isn't just about essential skills. While you'll hopefully soon be working towards the same aims and goals, it's almost inevitable that your personalities and life experience will give you different priorities and preferences. For example, one of us is particularly astute about the financial side of business and constantly aims to do fewer gigs for higher income. The other is happy to do a higher volume of work for less money, and places high priority on increasing his contacts and business network. (If you've been paying attention throughout this book, there probably won't be any doubt in your mind which of us each of those sentences refers to!) Each of us has realised the power that lies in different activities and priorities, and we now place higher value on e.g. careful money management and non-stop networking.

IMPROVED PLANNING

If you have any doubt about this, try first of all drawing up a mind map on your own. Then get together with someone else in your business network to work on the same mind map together. We can bet you anything that, no matter how long or hard you had thought independently about the core bubble and everything else connected to it, a huge number of new bubbles will appear when you collaborate with someone else. When you mind map together with your buddy on a regular basis, you will come up with better and more thorough ideas around any subject, and better ways to plan towards your ideal goals.

ACCOUNTABILITY

You must already know how much more motivated you feel to achieve personal goals such as weight loss or improved fitness when you are part of a group or working with a friend to reach a goal. Conversely, it's very easy to set goals for yourself and then postpone or ignore them when you're working on your own.

As soon as you start working together in your Buddy Up – defining goals, developing strategies and allotting tasks – you will feel super-motivated by the automatic and mutual accountability. You will want to keep working hard to maintain your Buddy Up relationship. You will be reporting back to each other on a regular basis, giving you set timeframes in which to complete tasks. And you won't only be congratulating yourself when you reach a goal, you will be sharing your success with and earning recognition from the person who is contributing most to your own success.

COMFORT FACTOR, COVERING JOBS

Stress is automatically reduced when you know someone who can help out if you can't cover a date or an order for a valued client. You will feel a constant and enhanced reduction in stress in a Buddy Up, knowing that you can trust your buddy to be reliable and to deliver the same standard of service. We also both collaborate with other high-quality magicians and infotainers, each of us bringing extra contacts to the group. In that group, we all benefit from increased workload and income, with more people networking for all of us, and with the comfort factor of knowing there's always someone else to cover a job when required.

SHARING RESOURCES

For most businesses, there are practical aspects that present financial challenges. A successful Buddy Up is very likely to allow each partner to benefit from sharing resources such as premises, training facilities, meeting rooms, venues, technology or equipment.

POSITIVE MINDSET AND OUTCOMES

No explanation needed here – just a list to remind you of the areas in which the Buddy Up System can lead to significant improvements, with direct benefits to your personal and business development.

ENERGY	MOTIVATION	COURAGE
ENTHUSIASM	WORKLOAD	CONNECTIVITY
INNOVATION	CONFIDENCE	INCOME

This section on our Buddy Up System is the longest in this book. See the next page for our mind map, which you can use to remind yourself of all the points you need to consider.

At the time of writing, we have known each other for only two years, and what we have achieved together still feels unbelievable. We have absolutely no doubt that, while we are both highly driven and resourceful, it is the Buddy Up System that has had the biggest impact. Our business output and income have more than quadrupled since we have combined forces, which is living proof of how powerful the Buddy Up System can be. Two people working together brings double the effort, knowledge and energy in the partnership, but the effect on innovation, enthusiasm, confidence and income is compounded over and over, giving significantly more than double the results.

We never stop looking for ways to improve everything we do, and the Buddy Up System has itself morphed from a positive approach to collaboration to the powerful business tool we have given you here. We're sure we'll find further improvements – from our own and other people's experiences – which we'll add to any future editions of this book. For now, we'd like to give credit to the very talented Richard Redding, who was Spencer's boss for many years, and who gave Spencer his first insight into the benefits of tactical collaboration.

Before Richard's interview, a quick word about the afterword, which follows this chapter. A standard afterword is usually a conclusion or summary, or a description of the origins of a book, but we've already told you all that. Our afterword adds an entirely different dimension – potentially to everything we have told you so far. Please don't overlook it.

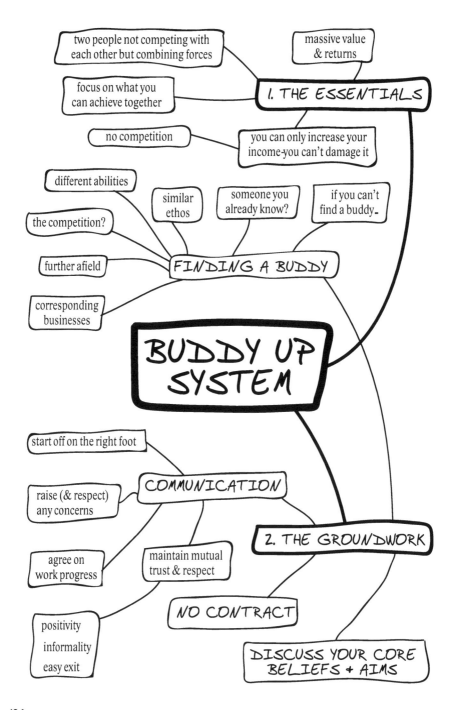

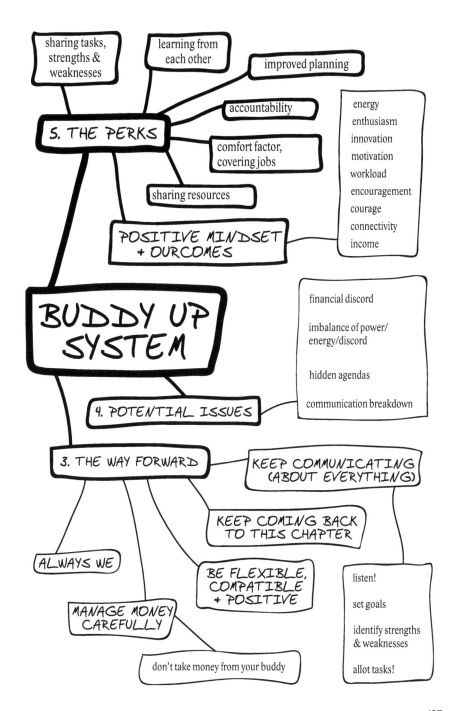

sharing tasks, strengths & weaknesses

learning from each other

improved planning

accountability

5. THE PERKS

comfort factor, covering jobs

sharing resources

energy
enthusiasm
innovation
motivation
workload
encouragement
courage
connectivity
income

POSITIVE MINDSET + OURCOMES

BUDDY UP SYSTEM

financial discord

imbalance of power/ energy/discord

hidden agendas

communication breakdown

4. POTENTIAL ISSUES

3. THE WAY FORWARD

KEEP COMMUNICATING (ABOUT EVERYTHING)

KEEP COMING BACK TO THIS CHAPTER

ALWAYS WE

BE FLEXIBLE, COMPATIBLE + POSITIVE

listen!

set goals

identify strengths & weaknesses

MANAGE MONEY CAREFULLY

don't take money from your buddy

allot tasks!

185

INTERVIEW WITH RICHARD REDDING
DIRECTOR OF SALES – MONTHIND CLEAN LLP

The Buddy up System started when we put together different teams that were tailored to clients' specific requirements. That was with our cleaning teams but also with the sales teams. With cleaners, in a large open-plan space, you'd have a team working together, rather than each person having their own area. You'd put them together as a team and they'd float through the different floors of a building, each doing their task. This increased productivity and improved team spirit, rather than cleaners working on their own for two to three hours.

In sales, rather than having set geographic areas for the sales people, we worked out their different strengths. As soon as we shared clients strategically, the figures markedly improved. It's just a case of thinking a little bit differently. For example, Spencer is very charismatic and polished, so he was very good in the City environment. Through his history with his father's cleaning company, he also had the ability to sell the 'grittier' types of contracts – he knows what it's like to roll his sleeves up.

Rules and regulations within a company – its processes and procedures – are there purely as a guideline. They've been set because they worked at a set time. In my opinion, all successful companies bend and flex with the changing climate and the changing requirements of their clients.

We always ask the client before the proposal meeting what they want from us. They'll say, 'You've got the agenda', and you'll say, 'Yes, I've seen the agenda. I can see you've got ten points covered, but what do you actually want to see from us from today? Is it focused on the operations, or on finance, or how much of it is going to be back-of-house – environmental or health and safety issues?' That way, you increase your strike rate, by going into the presentation fully prepared. If you know the half-dozen questions they're going to ask you, you can prepare your answers to all those questions rather than winging it. Although, winging it is something Spencer's very good at!

My background is advertising, and the key is to stand out. You've got to stand out in a positive or proactive way. Obviously, if you stand out for the wrong reasons, you've lost the bid. But if you stand out well, your pitch will be well received. If you're well prepared, if the client is genuine, he'll go into that presentation thinking, 'This crowd coming in has actually taken time to find out what I want to see'.

There are lots of things that contribute to the success rate. Like when it comes to discussing the proposal; they've spent two weeks putting it together – at least have the courtesy to read it. Mark it up visually, say with brightly coloured sticky tabs, so the client can see that you've actually read it. If you ask a question that's answered in the proposal, you're not going through to the presentation. Preparation is critical to winning a bid . . . if you want to win it. If you just want to sit around for a couple of weeks reading comics, don't bother preparing!

Something Spencer always did was to put two prices on the table. That way, you're almost adding another bidder to the table and increasing your percentage chance of a win. Say, if the client now has four prices to choose from, even though each of your prices only has a 25 per cent chance of winning, together they have 50 per cent. It also gives you another stand-out, if you're the only company that's bothering to put two quotes together. Those two prices could be based on different factors, such as cost versus service level. I think it's always good to take a colleague along, so you'll be looking at it from two different viewpoints. I haven't come across a client yet that objects to that. Again, you've taken time to come at their job from two different angles. Now the client is benefiting from two different prices, and two different options or styles.

No matter how long you've been in the industry, you have more to learn. We've all got job titles, but my business card has only my name and number on it. I know that, unless the cleaners turn up at five in the morning and clean the muck from the back of your sink, I'm nothing in this business. Ultimately, we're a service industry, so the most important person is the cleaner we put in. It's like the TV programme *Back to the Floor* – with any new salesperson, on day one they turn up with their new suit and satchel, say all the right things and pick up a laptop and a car. Day two, I want them out cleaning toilets with one of the operators. First of all, that wins over the operator, that this isn't just some guy in a suit in an office; secondly, once you've cleaned a toilet, you won't underestimate how long it takes.

Spencer's dad is charming and hard-working. He started off cleaning grease from axles underneath lorries. He did another lorry, another lorry; then the yard, the toilets, the canteen, then another building down the road; and grew his business like that. When Spencer needed pocket money, he'd have his hand down lorry drivers' toilets.

Spencer always was an extremely talented salesperson, even if he was too confident at first. I know exactly when he changed – it was when he buddied up with Lisa, his wife. Then when his eldest daughter was born, the world fell into place for him. Talking about this now, I'm realising how the buddying-up system contributes to many different strings of your life.

Spencer and I had an awful lot of fun. I've got salespeople who are turning in the same numbers as him, but I miss his camaraderie and his honesty. Spencer has that charismatic charm – he could walk around in a pair of wellies and a bin sack and he'd still look good. It's actually quite annoying! I think we're very similar in thinking that you don't need to make a friend in everyone you meet, but there's no need to turn them into an enemy. I think the morals that we've both been brought up with by our respective fathers are based on strong family principles – politeness, good manners and hard work – but whatever happens, you've got to have a laugh. It's tough out there but you've got to enjoy it. If you don't enjoy it, you'll get dragged down and you'll drag other people down with you. Trust is vital – it might take five years to build up to a level of trust, but only five minutes to break it, then you'll never get that same level of trust back.

When Spencer said he wanted to go into magic, I didn't think it was the right decision at the time, but he was so passionate about it. It was hard for him for a while, but look at him now. And Spencer's a proud man – he never went cap in hand to his dad, which would have been very easy to do.

AFTERWORD

You'll notice this isn't a normal afterword. We've already told you enough about our reasons for writing this book and how we developed our ideas. The only point we want to highlight as a conclusion is that, by reading this far, you will have absorbed over 70 sections of motivational tips and advice. There have been whole books written about at least half of those subjects. As we promised in the introduction, our aim from the start has been to deliver straightforward and condensed advice. We'll be intrigued if anyone tries to summarise the key points of this book.

This afterword goes in a different direction from the rest of the book, for two reasons:

There is concrete, practical reasoning behind everything we've told you so far. The following section is abstract and unprovable, yet it's something we both 100% believe in. It's something Spencer applies to just about everything he does, so he's going to write it from his perspective.

SPENCER: BELIEVE THE UNBELIEVABLE

I've always been ready to believe that there are forces at play in our lives that are beyond scientific proof. I haven't studied quantum physics and I don't believe in superstitions, ghosts or psychic powers. But as soon as I started to believe in positive energy and the law of attraction, I experienced significant improvements in just about everything I put my hand to.

If you are willing to be openminded, no matter how much you already believe in abstract influences, I hope this will help to change or further enhance your way of thinking.

You might like to start with some inspirational YouTube videos around this subject, by searching under 'Jim Carrey visualisation' and 'celebrities law of attraction'. There are many great books out there about this type of belief system, but those short YouTube clips were enough reassurance for me that I'm not insane! There are countless incredibly successful people out there who have beliefs similar to mine.

There will always be people who can offer you proof of how visualisation and positive thinking don't work. Don't listen to them. Just start to believe (100%) that there are no limits to what you can and will achieve, and I am 100% sure that you will very soon start to notice big differences.

You can't simply think more positively, sit back and wait for things to happen. You have to keep working hard, but that goes hand in hand with harnessing positive energy – knowing you will achieve more will immediately give you the motivation to do more, and vice versa. When Dr Sophie Shotter shared some of her business secrets with us, she said towards the end of the interview, 'I'm a firm believer that basically the Universe has our back, that there's a plan for all of us. That doesn't mean that you should just sit back and coast through life – you shouldn't. If something bad happens to you, what's making it bad is how you're thinking about it. If you just get your head around that and accept it – accept that it's happening for a reason and that there is something better on the other side of that – life becomes so much easier.'

What is there to lose? Here's my take on three things I've found most successful so far.

KARMA
Even the smallest act of generosity or helpfulness will one day bring something good back to you. It could be a direct payback – someone

doing you a favour because you helped them out – but more often than not it happens indirectly. We both honestly believe that giving out positive energy, doing the right thing and helping other people will very soon bring you positive returns.

Do everything positive you can think of (without e.g. bankrupting yourself) over the next year, then contact us if you are honestly convinced you haven't enjoyed positive returns.

100% SELF-BELIEF

Take your self-belief to a different level. This is similar to what we told you in Chapter 3, but it's no longer about gradually increasing your confidence. It's about deciding to develop an **instant new level of 100% self-belief.**

Unless you are willing now to believe 100% that this is possible, keep the intention in your mind and wait until a calm, happy and successful point in your life, when you are genuinely willing to believe that this is possible. It's absolutely fine if it takes you a few attempts – as long as you believe it's possible and really want this for yourself, you *will* be able to do it.

All you need to do is decide that there are NO limits to what you can and will achieve. Decide that there is no longer any room for self-doubt, and that there is no going back. Once you have made this decision, no matter what happens, you will have joined an incredible new journey forward. You will be able to achieve anything you set your mind to, and you'll do everything you need to do to get where you want to be.

ACCOUNTABILITY

I use unconventional techniques and approaches every single day to boost my motivation and my outcomes.

One example:
I decide I want to secure at least £2k of new business for next year by the end of this week. So I decide that I am going to buy a great (but expensive) new Lego set for my daughters, for us to work on together next weekend. Lego is their favourite thing at the moment, and we all love having time out together. Now I set myself a simple goal: if I get the £2k new business by Friday, I'll buy the Lego set; if I don't, I can't.

There is no room for cheating in this system. If I reach a goal but don't get whatever I've promised myself or someone else, the system will backfire and I'll miss the next few goals I set myself. Or if I fail to reach the goal I've set, then cheat and buy whatever I've promised myself or someone else, I will then lose at least the same amount of business. It might not be associated with that week, but throughout the month I'll get a series of cancellations or fail to get gigs I normally would. All of a sudden, it's as if someone is saying, 'I gave what you asked for, but you didn't follow through at the other end.' Or 'You didn't reach the target, but you still rewarded yourself.'

The same goes for smaller, daily targets. For example: I decide I need to send 50 emails to prospects by midday, after which I can go out to my favourite coffee shop to buy a coffee and sandwich. If I don't achieve that goal, I've missed that window. Then I can't even set myself a goal for the afternoon, or I have to double my target for the morning after, i.e. 100 emails before I can get the coffee and sandwich.

One of my favourite (or least favourite) examples is curry versus jacket potato. For me, there are few meals that can beat a good curry, and I seriously detest jacket potatoes. You guessed it – if I reach a set target by the end of the week, I reward myself with a curry from my favourite Indian restaurant, with all the sundries and a couple of side dishes. If I don't reach the target, I'm going to have to head to the supermarket to buy a massive, ugly potato and a can of beans. People who know me well enough don't bother asking how my day's gone, they just ask what I'm having for dinner that night.

I set myself specific goals and rewards for every new project or timeframe. Whatever I do, I have to make peace with myself that I have set a challenging goal. For every investment, I set myself a target in order to balance the books or justify the expense. Even if I've got money in the bank to cover a new investment, I still create a new goal first, to raise the money from a different source, before making that investment.

I'll stop with the examples and explanations. We promised you no waffle, but I needed to give you concrete ideas of my genuine beliefs and motivation strategies, which enable me to achieve more than I ever would otherwise.

Whether you already believe in some sort of spirituality or are 100% sure that science explains everything on this planet, we now have to put you centre stage. NOW YOU NEED TO TAKE ACTION.

We trust that you have been inspired by what you have read in this book, but the real value comes only when you follow the steps we have given you. As we said in the introduction, some of the steps are easy and others more challenging, but none are impossible. At the very least, keep the checklist on page 166 close to you . . . as soon as you are able to tick off most of the boxes on that list, you will know that our system guarantees personal and business success.

We both genuinely wish you every success in reaching your own new levels of extraordinary potential.

ACKNOWLEDGEMENTS

Do many people normally read acknowledgements pages and remember all the names and comments? Please just make a mental note to refer back to this page whenever you need a brilliant and reliable person from one of the professions in this mind map. These are friends and associates who all helped with the research and creation of this book, whose abilities and business skills we 100% recommend.

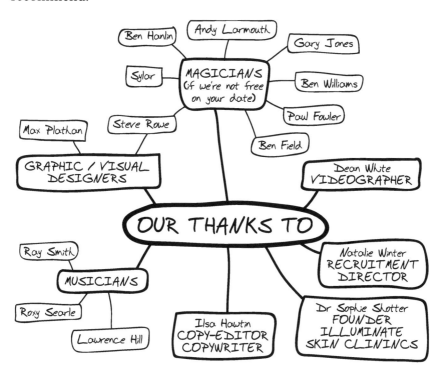

The only people we need to thank separately are all our family members – our parents, wives and children. And Trevor Liley and Richard Redding. All of these people helped us to get where we are today.

48175712R00125

Printed in Poland
by Amazon Fulfillment
Poland Sp. z o.o., Wrocław